In Celebration
of Wine and Life

In Celebration of Wine and Life

THE FASCINATING STORY OF WINE AND CIVILIZATION

with art reproductions from

The Wine Museum of San Francisco

THE CHRISTIAN BROTHERS COLLECTION

By Richard B. Lamb
and
Ernest G. Mittleberger
with a Foreword by
Alfred Fromm

Published by The Wine Appreciation Guild
San Francisco
1980

© Copyright 1980 by The Wine Museum of San Francisco

Published in the United States of America in 1980
by THE WINE APPRECIATION GUILD
  1377 Ninth Avenue
  San Francisco, California 94122

Revised edition.

Library of Congress Cataloging in Publication Data

Lamb, Richard B.
    In celebration of wine and life.
  1. Wine and wine making—Pictorial works
  2. Wine and wine making—History
I.   Mittelberger, Ernest G., joint author II. Title
Library of Congress Catalogue Card Number: 80-51213
ISBN   0932664-12-1   (hardbound)
ISBN   0932664-13-X   (paperbound)

This song of mine
Is a song of the vine
To be sung by the glowing embers
Of wayside inns
When the rain begins
To darken the drear Novembers.

Henry Wadsworth Longfellow
1854

Acknowledgements

There is little room in the realm of wine lore for personal vanity, for the sum of our knowledge is an overwhelming total of minutiae that have accumulated almost from the beginning of time. Nowhere is this more apparent than in California, where the present work was assembled and where the state itself, through its century-old university, has played such a dominant role in the improvement of grape-growing and winemaking techniques.

Anyone who writes about wine — and, indeed, anyone who enjoys drinking it — owes a large debt to members of the faculty in the University of California's Department of Viticulture and Enology on the Davis campus. Your chroniclers acknowledge that debt, for they have drawn freely upon the knowledge generated by these dedicated scientists, notably Professors Maynard A. Amerine, Harold P. Olmo, and Albert J. Winkler.

They are indebted also to Dr. Frank A. Norick, principal anthropologist at the Lowie Museum of Anthropology on the university's Berkeley campus; and to Messrs. Hugh Cook and Terrance McInnes of The Wine Institute in San Francisco.

Deserving special gratitude because they have "lived" with this book through its sometimes painful hours of gestation are Mrs. Natalie Fromm, director of exhibits at The Wine Museum of San Francisco; Mr. Robert Emory Johnson, its art consultant; and Miss Emily Newell of the museum staff, who helped to select, authenticate, and caption the illustrations.

Need it be added, in justice to all these good people, that the fallible judgments expressed herein are those of the authors?

The photographic illustrations are the work primarily of Mr. Jim Goldberg, who photographed most of the three-dimensional objects; Mr. Lloyd Hryciw, who photographed many of the prints and drawings; and Mr. O. E. Nelson, who produced the black-and-white photographs of glasses. Included also are photographs by Messrs. Charles Davis, John Henshall, and Joe Schopplein.

R. L.

E. G. M.

ACKNOWLEDGEMENTS FOR THE REVISED EDITION

In the preparation of this revised edition, much credit goes to Mary M. Rodgers, for her thorough and detailed editing of the text, to Max Silten, for revision of the design and quality of the book's presentation, and to Maurice T. Sullivan, for his professional advice and encouragement.

E.G.M.

Contents

Foreword

This book first appeared to commemorate the birth of The Wine Museum of San Francisco. In a larger sense, however, that first printing and the present revised edition are a commemoration of many lives—my own included—dedicated to the art and pleasure of wine. The Wine Museum of San Francisco is the only public museum of its kind in the United States. This volume, illustrated with many drawings, prints, and photographs from the museum's collection of artworks, is a small tribute to the history and romance of wine.

The museum is the realization of a personal dream of many years. The Fromm family have been vintners for nearly two centuries. My late partner, Franz W. Sichel, also was deeply involved in wine and the arts; for generations his family, too, has been a celebrated name in wine. His warm humanity, his discerning taste, is kept alive in this museum by one of the world's finest collections of glass drinking-vessels — beautiful, rare, and costly — assembled by Franz over many years.

The Wine Museum is an ideal forum in which to present together a collection of art and rare books dealing with the delights of wine. Its offerings span the centuries and are the work of artists, craftsmen, and writers who sensed the uniqueness of wine as a symbol — a bridge between God and man.

It is perhaps inevitable that my wife, Hanna, and I would want to share our pleasure in the collection with as many people as possible. My family has long been sensitive to the inspirational role of wine — in music, painting and sculpture, graphics and literature. Our own lives have been woven in and out of the arts, moving to and fro among the business of wine, the enticements of fine art, and the aesthetics of wine. For winemaking — as we learned it and as we believe in it — is an art in itself that has spoken to men through the ages.

To trace the origins of The Wine Museum of San Francisco, we must begin with the Franconia wine country of Bavaria. There my great-grandfather lived, a village schoolmaster with a small stipend that could not clothe, feed, and shoe his family of eleven children. He became involved in the problems of his neighbors, who were for the most part grape growers and wine-makers. Yet, they had no great winemaking skill and made wine the way it had always been made by their forefathers; sometimes the wine turned out well, sometimes it was poor. My great-grandfather helped them make better wine and, as the quality of the wine improved, a small trade developed. Gradually most of Bavaria became familiar with the Franconia wines. In 1810 my great-grandfather attached his name, N. Fromm, to the family winemaking business.

Later my grandfather took it over, and the reputation of Fromm wines continued to grow. My father, Max, was only thirteen when his father died. He was the only son of the family and had to leave school to earn his two older sisters' dowries. Although he had no formal education, he was outstandingly intelligent and possessed great drive; he was in his manhood a wine taster renowned throughout the land. During the ensuing thirty years, he built a thriving business in Kitzingen in the heart of the wine country, and was instrumental in organizing the neighboring vintners into a cooperative that grew the Franconia wines so greatly esteemed throughout Germany. Max Fromm, a civic-minded man and adviser to the government on many questions of viticulture and enology, won the official title, *Kommerzienrat* (Counselor of Commerce), an honor bestowed upon those important businessmen who gave of their talents to the country.

In 1928, N. Fromm — Winegrowers, Vintners, and Shippers — moved its headquarters to Bingen on the Rhine, the center of a district producing fine Riesling, Sylvaner, and Müller-Thurgau grapes. The town is so steeped in wine that corkscrews are known everywhere in Germany as "Bingen pencils"; corkscrews, of course, are a principal tool of the winemaking business.

I began my apprenticeship at fifteen, when I had completed the equivalent of high school. This was customary for a boy going into a particular field, and I learned all the phases of the wine business before entering a viticultural college. My apprenticeship was with one of the Rhineland's largest wine firms. One of my earliest duties was to prepare for the daily wine tastings of the senior staff; I set the samples on a revolving table and prepared the glasses for the tasters. The senior partner took a liking to me and occasionally asked me to taste a wine. Soon I joined the older men at the tasting table and sampled wines with them every day. By the time I was eighteen, I prided myself on my reliability as a wine taster. After I had served my apprenticeship, I attended the viticultural college at Geisenheim, which was then the leading European institution of its kind, and upon graduation I entered our family firm in 1923.

Each day between noon and one o'clock, I joined my father and three other men — all authorities on wine — in the tasting room. The hour was chosen so that we would have empty stomachs — we breakfasted early — and fresh palates. Of course, none of us smoked. To keep our palates neutral, we would take nothing but warm water and a bit of white bread. We sampled from sixty to eighty wines from our large cellars to determine if they needed more time in the casks or were ready to be bottled. What a pleasure it was to follow a wine over the years from its infancy to its prime! We looked upon our wines as our children, and we felt the pride of parents.

Our firm had a fine laboratory equipped to analyze a wine, but we knew that no test was a substitute for a good wine-man's palate. Tasting is still the only sure way to know if a wine tastes right, looks right, and smells right. It is, however, one of the vintner's most strenuous and important tasks, demanding both tremendous concentration and tranquility. To get into the proper frame of mind, I would prepare myself about an hour before the tasting — perhaps by taking a stroll through the surrounding vineyards, or by visiting the cellars. If I allowed myself to be interrupted by telephone calls or distracted by business matters, I could not trust my judgment as completely.

Over the years the wines a good taster has

experienced become etched in his memory. He must remember the character of a certain wine before it went into the cask, how it developed there and subsequently in the bottle, and apply his memory to each new wine before him. I can still recall the taste of a rare wine we enjoyed at my sister's wedding when I was fifteen years old. It was a 1911 Hochheimer Domdechaney Trockenbeerenauslese, and when the bottle was opened the entire room smelled like a bouquet of flowers. It had a deep golden hue, and we drank it from small crystal glasses.

The taste of a wine is difficult to put into words, but I readily learned the descriptive language then in use. For example, we would say a wine is pleasant "but it has no tail," which simply meant that it did not linger on and that something was missing. Another wine might be called "a great lady," with an implication of nobility and breeding; or be described as being "like a baby's bottom," firm but soft. And, when a wine was an attractive bluffer but lacked real substance, we called it a "harlot." It is difficult to give the precise translation of many of the German words we used during these tastings.

In 1923, inflation was at its worst in Germany, and my father decided that we must begin to export our wines. I was delegated to go to Denmark, later to Sweden and Norway, and in 1925 to Finland, when that country repealed its Prohibition.

I was young and enthusiastic, and relished introducing new people to our good wines. My younger brother, Paul, sold our wines in Poland, Holland, and Belgium, and by 1933 — the year the Nazis came into power — N. Fromm had cellars and offices in Saarbrücken, Amsterdam, Prague, and London. In ten short years, our wines were selling in sixty countries, but it soon became apparent that the Fromm family could not continue to live under the Hitler regime.

Even for an export-oriented firm such as ours, America seemed as far away as the moon. But my father decided that one of us should go there, so I — the older of the two sons in the firm — was chosen. I arrived in New York in December, 1933, immediately after the end of Prohibition. How awed I was by the size of this country, by the vitality of its cities, and by the diversity of its people. Heeding my father's advice to "get out of New York," I bought a used Ford and explored the land. I went from Maine to Florida, saw all the southern states, the Midwest, and the West Coast. I made a point of taking side trips to view the many scenic sights of the country — Niagara Falls, the Carlsbad Caverns, the Grand Canyon, Yellowstone Park, the Rocky Mountains, and Yosemite. I got a deep impression of this land and its people, and I determined to stay here even though the wine trade in the United States did not at that time appear too promising.

Many people then thought it was a little "sissy" to drink wine, especially right after Prohibition; the average American, it seemed, would drink nothing but hard liquor. Despite this obstacle, I was joined by other pioneering wine men from Germany, France, Italy, and Spain. We were all traveling missionaries in those days, preaching the glories of wine.

A few years later, the small firm of importers acting as N. Fromm's distributor in the United States asked me to become a partner. During 1936 and 1937 I went repeatedly to Europe to buy wine, and each trip strengthened my conviction that war was very near. As war would certainly cut off our access to European wines, I realized we would have to begin growing our own quality wines in the United States. With that thought in mind, I went to California and visited every winery in the state, among them Mont La Salle, the Napa Valley winery of The Brothers of The Christian Schools. After much discussion, The Brothers and I agreed that the time had come to develop a premium California wine, and to market it in a new way.

I stayed at The Christian Brothers monastery for four months, and together with Brother John and Brother Timothy tasted every barrel of wine in their cellars. We made our marketing plans and my firm was appointed sole distributor, a fruitful relationship that still survives after decades. Early in 1938 we introduced a line of

The Christian Brothers wines and did something new at the time: We fixed a uniform price and sold all our wine in bottles bearing The Christian Brothers label, rather than in bulk. That way the consumer would know that the wines shipped under The Christian Brothers label had been bottled at the monastery and had met The Brothers' high standards of quality. We were thus able to establish a brand, and the consumer was thereby benefited.

That was the business side of wine, and there was much toil and financial worry connected with it. But, as Brother John liked to say, we were also "blessed from above with good fortune."

As the years progressed, my three brothers followed me to the United States. Norman, an attorney by profession, but a music historian at heart, also became associated with our firm. Until his death two years ago, Norman's life was divided almost equally between wine and music. He was the founder and president of the San Francisco Chamber Music Society and the originator of the summer concert series, Music at the Vineyards, at Saratoga, California. My younger brother Paul, a wine importer in Chicago for many years, founded The Fromm Music Foundation at Harvard University, which is probably the foremost institutional sponsor of modern music. My twin brother Herbert, who lives in Boston, is a well-known composer of liturgical and secular music and a writer of poetry and essays.

Later, my parents and my sisters, Fridl, Joan, and Margaret, also came to the United States. Once again the family was united, this time on American soil. Almost until his death at eighty-four, my father tasted wines daily, ever the stern taskmaster and sage adviser.

All this brings us again to the "why" of The Wine Museum. Unlike my brothers, I cannot make music nor can I paint or write poetry. But I have been fortunate to be in a profession that is close indeed to an art, and allows me to feel that I have contributed to the pleasures of life. At the same time, our association with The Brothers of The Christian Schools has given me a great sense of satisfaction in that it has enabled me to help forward the educations of thousands of young men. The principal source of The Brothers' teaching funds in the western United States is the sale of their premium wines.

A point that was always emphasized in our family was that one must contribute something to one's country; I am convinced that you cannot be a good citizen unless you so contribute. There is also the matter of pride: I would like to be remembered for having played some part in the birth of the American quality-wine business. Thus, thirteen or fourteen years ago, the idea for a wine museum began to take shape, a museum that would exalt the harmony of wine and the arts. It would enable us to share with the public some of the joys we have had in the art of making wine and in the fine arts that have celebrated wine for thousands of years.

Wine and the arts have greatly enriched man's lives throughout history. We say a small prayer that this book and The Wine Museum of San Francisco will allow many thousands to share that enrichment with us.

ALFRED FROMM
San Francisco, California

Introduction

"Wine," said Goethe, "rejoices the heart of men, and joy is the mother of virtue."

If the German philosopher and poet was exhilarated by the wines of the eighteenth and nineteenth centuries, how much more would his heart have been gladdened by those of the twentieth century! Of these wines it can truly be said that rejoicing the heart of men is only one of their many virtues. Wine improves the disposition, restores the spirit, dispels sorrow, generates laughter, overcomes timidity.

Wine evokes friendship, stimulates conversation and appetite, adds zest to a meal, replenishes human energy, stabilizes health, and aids in convalescence.

To this long but probably incomplete list of wine's virtues, we may add the special enjoyment we find in tasting and comparing individual wines. Some people even make a hobby of collecting choice wines. They study the names and characteristics of wines from the world's most honored winemaking areas, they taste and sniff and gaze into the haunting depths of these rare wines, and the discoveries they make embellish their conversational versatility.

Not the least of wine's virtues, as the illustrations in this book so vividly show, is that it inspires the artist. Yet the poet, the painter, the musician, the sculptor, and the dramatist do not require the connoisseur's highly specialized knowledge of wine to bestir their creative impulses. Nor do most of us need that reservoir of innumerable, intimate details in order to enjoy wine. An eager lover, wine does not demand to be wooed; it is there in the glass, an invitation to a warm embrace.

There are, however, some basic facts about wine that, once known, can enliven the conversation that often blossoms around an open bottle, and enlightened conversation, like compatible food, is a complement to the enjoyment of wine.

One of the goals of this book is to present a store of basic information about wine: what it is and where it originates. Another aim is to provide a suitable showcase for the illustrations, many of which are reproductions of original artworks from The Christian Brothers Collection on exhibit at The Wine Museum of San Francisco. Some of them have not been on public view anywhere in this country, and the publication of this volume marks the first time that all of them have been brought together under one roof.

That is why this book attempts to relate wine to Western culture, to the mythology of ancient Greece and Rome, and to its ecclesiastical heritage reaching back to pre-Biblical times. It's also why it tells a little about how and where good wine grapes are grown and how wine is made and aged.

Grape growing and winemaking are essentially the same today as they were at the time of the Romans. Now, as then, selected vines are planted and cared for, the grapes are harvested and crushed, and the juice becomes wine through Nature's process of fermentation. Over the centuries, grape growers and winemakers have developed small refinements and improvements in the procedure so as to help Nature along. In total, these refinements have been so extensive that the everyday wine we select from the merchant's shelf today is far superior to anything our forebears could buy at any price.

The fundamentals and techniques of grape growing and winemaking in the various producing regions on all continents are much more alike than they are dissimilar. Of course, there are differences in customs and practices, but the difference between a premium-quality winery and a mass-production winery in the same growing area is often greater than the difference between the winemaking practices of, say, the United States and France, Italy, or Germany.

The most important variations can be sensed in the final products you raise to your lips. Mostly the differences come from the grape and its pedigree: its "family," and where and how it was grown. Other characteristics come from the way the grape juice was made into wine — the process of "vinification" — and how the wine was cared for afterward, before it reached your table.

Wine is a complex beverage. It contains so many natural substances that scientists are still discovering new facts about it. This complexity accounts for the vast number of producers and the great variety of wines available to us. There are more producers and marketers of wine than of any other food or beverage. More than ten thousand variously labeled wines are offered for sale in the American marketplace. Nobody can know them all, and no book describes them all.

Because of the vagaries of the weather there, vintage years are important in regard to most European wines, especially those of high quality, but their relative values change constantly and never apply to all the wines of a given region, let alone a given country. A collector, therefore, must be certain that his wine merchant supplies him with the most recent vintage chart. Each successive vintage chart records the changes caused by the aging process, which improves different wines at varying speeds and eventually leads them over the top and downhill. The 1952 Saint-Pierre Medoc, to pick a name, could well have enjoyed distinction until 1969. That particular wine, though, then began to decline; a 1969 vintage chart would therefore misguide a buyer. The safest guide in selecting wines is the good name of a reliable vintner.

Harold Grossman, one of the recognized writers on wine and other beverages, compiled a vintage chart that goes back to 1926. Yet he writes: "I abhor a slavish devotion to vintage charts . . . The relative quality of the wines of any vintage is necessarily very general. Some good wines are made in even 'poor' years and not all wines turn out 'great' in the great years."

To the sensory delights of wine is added an intellectual dimension of the sort that is found in fine paintings, sculptures, poems, or in a great concerto. We become subtly aware of the unique elation that wine can contribute to our lives. In the moments when we view the brilliant wine in the glass and capture its aroma and taste, the image of all we know about wine and associate with it flashes on our mental screen. The more beautiful the experiences we have stored up, the more delightful is this image and the more it enhances our enjoyment.

This mental photomontage is constantly enriched by the scenes we absorb — in books and pictures, in other artworks, and even in wine labels.

We not only enjoy the wine for its own qualities but also compare it with wines we had in the past, and half-consciously contemplate the long way the wine traveled before it reached the glass — from vine and grape through cask and bottle. We may have actually seen the sequence in the vineyard and winery or observed it in works of art.

Artists of past and present times have received inspiration from every step in the growing, making, and drinking of wine. This book contains many of their images, in which they depict the annual cycle of grape growing in the vineyards, culminating in joyful harvest festivals, the crushing and pressing of grapes to yield the juice Nature transforms into wine, and the slumbering and aging of wine in casks of many shapes, handmade by the members of the cooper's guild. Our artists even follow the wine from cool cellars through sunny countrysides to inns and other gathering places where cheerful drinkers celebrate life with wine, music, and laughter.

Art, poetry, and music offer an accompaniment to the melody that wine plays in our celebration of life. Anytime, anywhere, in the intimate company of loved ones and of friends or at large banquets or festivals, in spring or autumn, under a shady tree on a warm Sunday afternoon, or in the evening by the fireplace as the cares of the busy day slip away, wine brings pleasure and contentment.

With wine we can celebrate whenever we so desire, and we can make any day a holiday. For the enjoyment of wine is a very personal experience; as we develop our own relationship to it, we discover new ways to appreciate it and to celebrate with it, ways far better than any "how-to" book can ever suggest. It is hoped that the many reproductions of wine-inspired artworks in this book will make a small contribution to the reader's very own celebration of wine and life.

RICHARD LAMB AND
ERNEST G. MITTELBERGER

INTRODUCTION FOR THE REVISED EDITION

The phenomenal growth of wine appreciation, wine growing, and wine drinking in America, has prompted the review, revision, and updating of *In Celebration of Wine and Life*. With the encouragement of the publisher, this revised edition also offers the reader superior quality reproductions of artworks in The Christian Brothers Collection and several other sources.

My co-author, Richard Lamb, died in 1978, and I greatly miss his conversation, wisdom, and inspiration. Yet, this book, as well as the multitude of his other writings, are perpetual memories to a wonderful, gifted, and kind man. I am sure he would be proud of this new edition.

ERNEST G. MITTELBERGER
San Francisco, California
June 1980

The Wine Museum of San Francisco

On January 22, 1980, six years had elapsed since the opening of The Wine Museum of San Francisco. During that time, more than eight hundred thousand visitors had enjoyed this unique exhibition of artistic expressions in appreciation of wine from earliest times to the present.

This museum is the first wine-in-the-arts museum in the Americas. It is devoted exclusively to telling the story of wine and its enjoyment through exhibits of traditional and modern sculpture, artifacts, fine drawings and original prints, rare books, and drinking vessels from the major wine growing regions of the world.

The exhibits are laid out by subject matter and each section contains both pictorial and three-dimensional art from past and present periods. Proceeding clockwise, the visitor moves from the section on the *Grape and Vine* to the *Vintage and Harvest*, then to *Winemaking and the Vintner*. The impressive section on wine vessels presents ancient amphorae, silver tankards and cups, and the beautiful, comprehensive glass exhibit. The section on *Wine in Mythology*, dominated by images of Bacchus/Dionysus, the god of wine, is followed by the *Celebration of Wine and Life*. It shows people in various countries and periods enjoying the drinking of wine.

A major feature in the museum is a display of the famed *Franz W. Sichel Glass Collection* on loan from the Franz W. Sichel Foundation. This assemblage spans nearly 2,000 years and includes drinking vessels from the Roman era to the present. It is, indeed, a "visual history" of the development of drinking vessels. One of the noteworthy pieces on view here is the Verzelini glass, dated 1590, one of six in existence.

To keep The Wine Museum of San Francisco a vital, living institution, temporary exhibits, each centering on a particular wine-related theme, have been mounted for the enjoyment of the visitor. These *Changing Exhibitions* have included "Wine in Opera," in recognition of the close relationship

between wine and music; "The Cooper's Art," the important adjunct to the vintner's art; "Daumier on Wine," an impressive collection of mid-nineteenth-century caricatures by the talented and satiric Frenchman, Honoré Daumier; "Thomas Jefferson and Wine in Early America," the museum's unique historical exhibit executed in honor of the nation's bicentennial celebration; "Bacchus Today," featuring "Fifty Years of Wine Cartoons from the New Yorker;" "2000 Years: Evolution of the Wine Bottle" tracing the development of the vessel which has become so important for the enjoyment of wine, and "Roots of Heaven: Wine and Religion from the Ancient World to the Present," depicting the role wine enjoys in the rituals and celebrations of the classical, Renaissance, and modern periods.

The core of the museum houses *The Alfred Fromm Rare Wine Books Library*, which consists of about one thousand volumes from 1550 to the present in seven languages. It is used by students, researchers, and wine writers. Two of the core's outer walls present twelve-foot-long historic illustrated charts, called *Histowalls;* one presents the story of "Wine and Civilization" covering 6,000 years, the other the history of "Wine in California" with a time span of about 250 years. Other wine-related subjects are presented on four free-standing Readers.

Recent gifts have enlarged the collections to the point where a *Traveling Exhibition* of 120 graphics could be assembled. It is shown in museums throughout the country under the title, "500 Years of Wine in the Arts."

The Wine Museum of San Francisco, presenting The Christian Brothers Collection of wine-in-the-arts, is open to visitors Tuesday through Saturday, between 11:00 and 5:00, Sunday, noon to 5:00. It is closed Mondays and major holidays. Admission to the museum is always free. It is located at 633 Beach Street, opposite The Cannery, near Fisherman's Wharf.

Amphorae, such as these Etruscan examples, were used for the aging, storing, and shipping of wine. These tapered earthenware jugs with two handles at the neck were designed to be buried in the cellars or fit into a special framework on board the transport ships. The Greek amphorae held around 8½ gallons and were closed with terra-cotta stoppers reinforced with vine leaves, bound with twine, and daubed with clay or pitch seals. Lowie Museum of Anthropology, University of California, Berkeley.

1 Ageless Vine

*I*n a world that teeters periodically on the brink of crisis, the serenity of the vine and the grape is a comfort. It bespeaks civility, stability, and tranquillity. As far back into the past as man can peer, the vines were there, yielding their fruit. Emperors rose in their might to rule the world, or a part of it, then after a time had to step aside for others. Yet, generation after generation, century after century, the vine has stood aloof to human folly, each summer delivering its grapes for man to eat or to spread in the sun until they become raisins, or to crush for their juice in his quest for wine.

How far back? One legend that is believed to have arisen in 3500 B.C. or earlier describes King Jamshid's affection for grapes. This ancient ruler of Sumer in southern Mesopotamia harvested the fruit and stored it away in earthen jars for his winter treats. To his chagrin, some of the grapes spoiled, and he pushed those jars to the rear. But a lady of the court tasted the fermented juice, liked it, sipped some more,

and curled up on her pallet for a nap. Hearing of this, Jamshid too tried it, and all his court, with understandable results. Thus, says the legend, came wine to Sumer. The Sumerians even adopted a goddess of the vine, and named her Gestin, meaning "Mother Vine Stock."

There is in the cuneiforms of ancient Babylonia the *Epic of Gilgamesh*, half of it still preserved, which relates the prowess of an early Sumerian king and sings with joy of the trellised grapevines in the vineyard of the goddess Siduri and of the precious fluid pressed from the fruit of her Tree of Life.

An Early Label

Archaeologists have unearthed evidence that the vine yielded its treasure to the earliest Egyptians, although wine evidently was then the drink of only the privileged few, the affluent. In restored murals we see the vines and the harvest, the workers tramping out the juice, the wine being served in saucerlike vessels. The diggings

An outgrowth of the utilitarian amphorae was the decorated amphora with a flat base. It could be placed on shelves rather than buried or leaned against the cellar walls, and because of its stable base could be brought to the table for service. This Corinthian amphora exhibits the Oriental palmette motif of the seventh century B.C. *5⅙″ high.* Lowie Museum of Anthropology, University of California, Berkeley.

have turned up examples of the two-handled jugs called amphorae carrying the legend, "Very good wine from the House of Aten" and "Wine of the Western Side," among others. No strangers to grade-labeling, the Egyptians distinguished the good from the not-so-good by inscribing *nfr* on the jar; premium-grade wine naturally was *nfr-nfr*. There is the inscription at Esna that in translation says:

> "This is the wine cellar,
> The place for the produce of the vine is in it.
> One is merry in it
> And the heart of him who goes forth from it rejoices."

From those ancient temple walls, tomb writings, and artifacts of Egypt, Mesopotamia, Syria, and Phoenicia, we learn that with the exception of water and possibly a primitive beer, wine may well have been the earliest-known curb to man's thirst. As between water and wine, incidentally, Paul in his first letter to Timothy, the Bishop of Ephesus, rendered a value judgment that endures in the Scriptures. To his "beloved son in the faith," the apostle wrote: "Drink no longer water, but use a little wine for thy stomach's sake and thine often infirmities."

But long before Paul's travels in the first century, long before his literary struggles to keep the flame of faith burning in the Ephesians, the Romans, the Corinthians, and the Thessalonians, the vine and the grape were well established in the civilizations that sprang to life on the shores

This small Syrian glass amphora from the second-fourth centuries A.D. is an example of the luxury glass containers produced for the service of special wines at the tables of the elite. 7¾″ high. Lowie Museum of Anthropology, University of California, Berkeley.

24

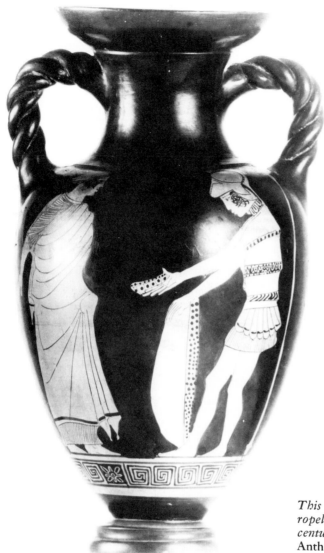

This example of red-figure amphorae has twisted ropelike handles and dates to around the fifth century B.C. *12½" high.* Lowie Museum of Anthropology, University of California, Berkeley.

of the Mediterranean. Wine became a staple of the commerce that made the Phoenicians a maritime power in the ports of Africa, Sicily, France, and Britain. Homer around 840 B.C. sang in his *Odyssey* and *Iliad* of earlier days that establish the vineyard as a fixture on every Greek farm that enjoyed suitable soil and climate.

A Gentle Persuasion

The Greeks didn't invent wine, of course, but in the long span of history they stand in the front rank of civilizations that embedded it in their culture. Indeed, the word *symposium* that is so prominent in our academic and economic lives comes to us from the meetings of

This is an example of a mid-fourth-century Greek red-figure calyx krater. Kraters were used for the mixing of wine with water, for the Greeks did not drink their wine straight. Lowie Museum of Anthropology, University of California, Berkeley.

This black-figure oinochoe or wine pitcher, dating to the last quarter of the fifth century B.C., shows the figure of Dionysus among grapevines between two satyrs who are carrying large eyes. 8⅔" high. Lowie Museum of Anthropology, University of California, Berkeley.

convivial spirits in early Greece — the warriors, sculptors, philosophers, statesmen — their gatherings for good talk, good wine, good music, and entertainment by comely dancing girls. Such a revel was known as a *symposion*, loosely translated from the Greek as "drinking party," or "drinking together." In this fashion, wine be-

came the catalyst that drew disparate elements of Greek culture together. Socrates said approvingly of the *symposion*, "If the servants constantly keep filling small cups, we are brought by the gentle persuasion of the wine to a gayer mood." Aristophanes agreed. "When men drink wine," he said, "they are rich. . . ." And Euripides

Kyathos, such as this late fifth-century B.C. *example, were used for ladling the wine out of kraters and pouring it into drinking cups. 3⅛" high.* Lowie Museum of Anthropology, University of California, Berkeley.

Opposite
This monumental red-figure volute krater dates from the last quarter of the fourth century B.C. *18" high.* Lowie Museum of Anthropology, University of California, Berkeley.

An Etruscan bucchero goblet. 5" high. Lowie Museum of Anthropology, University of California, Berkeley.

delivered this salute: "Where there is no wine, love perishes, and everything else that is pleasant to man."

Yet another word in our vocabulary that relates the early Greek to his propensity for wine is *bacchanal*. In fact, there's a whole family of words derived from the name Bacchus that the Greeks gave to their god of wine. Bacchus, known alternately as Dionysus, played a role that deserves closer inspection than is possible in a fast sweep of history. The god and the cult that grew up around him will be considered in Chapter II.

The wines of that era probably bore little resemblance to those available to us. The Athenian vintner and his counterparts in Byblos and Thrace, and on the fertile islands of Lesbos and Chios, produced a formidable drink, often high in alcohol by our standards and usually lacking in subtlety of taste. The Greeks didn't always drink it that way, though. It was the custom in convivial gatherings for the host to pour a few drops of the pure wine as a toast to the gods, then declare the dilution standards for the session — so many parts of water to one part of wine. Dilution not only dulled the sharp edge of the wine but enlarged the guest's staying power. Most of the Greek wine was made from sun-ripened grapes heavy with sugar; high in popularity was Pramnian wine, made from the sirupy juice that dripped from very ripe grapes before they were pressed. Some vintners used raisins dried from their wine grapes to produce a very sweet, very potent wine that was probably about 17 percent alcohol.

Vine cuttings went with the Greeks when, in the eighth century B.C., they expanded their horizon to embrace Magna Graecia in southern Italy, Sicily, Dalmatia, and North Africa. It is recorded that pre-Caesar Gaul, long before it became France, got its first taste of wine from the Greek merchants and seamen, who around 600 B.C. founded Massilia — today's Marseilles — and carried their wines up the Rhône River as far as Arles and Nîmes.

Itinerant Vines

Greek culture had strong impact in Italy. Not only the poetry and the drama of Athens were

This Etruscan kantharos is of bucchero, or gray ware, and bears an incised pattern of human profiles. 4½″ high. Lowie Museum of Anthropology, University of California, Berkeley.

embraced in the settlements along the Adriatic and Tyrrhenian coasts, but the vine cuttings, too; and by the time Rome turned on the Greeks and sacked Corinth in 146 B.C. the coastal Italians had cultivated a tidy wine industry. Within a century, Julius Caesar was to fling his legions into the Gallic Wars and bring the three parts of Gaul under the umbrella of the Roman Empire, beginning an era of pre-eminence for Rome that was to last two hundred years.

These were momentous events on the pages of history. They spanned decades, centuries even, when the cultivation of vines for their grapes and wines must have seemed a matter deserving low priority, if any at all, on the scale of human values.

Rome was already in decline as a world power when Constantine I moved the capital to Byzantium in A.D. 330 and changed its name to Con-stantinople, leading to an east-west split in the empire. Five hundred years after Caesar's assassination, the last vestige of "his" empire, the western part, slipped out of sight. The Byzantine — or East Roman — Empire was to endure until 1453, when Mohammed II seized Constantinople on the site of ancient Byzantium.

Political and military conquest may have seemed the greatest hazards confronting the empire in the days after Caesar's nephew Augustus had succeeded him. In fact, a new force was astir in the world, and it was to give Augustus, Nero, and others some sleepless nights. This force was Christianity, the doctrine of an obscure Judean carpenter's son and the motley band of fishermen, laborers, scribes, and peasants who followed him. They, too, were to play a part in the popularization of wine, a role that will also be discussed in the following chapter.

An archaic Greek Attic black-figure kylix, an elegantly simple drinking cup from the mid-sixth century B.C. *Lowie Museum of Anthropology, University of California, Berkeley.*

This Greek Attic red-figured skyphos drinking cup is attributed to the mid-fifth century B.C. *7⅔" high.* Lowie Museum of Anthropology, University of California, Berkeley.

Encircling the Sea

However dourly the Men of Destiny may have viewed the Middle Ages, it's reassuring to note that viticulture thrived not only in the three parts of Caesar's Gaul but around the perimeter of the Mediterranean as well. Ausonius, writing in the fourth century, rejoiced in the vineyards that covered the hills along the Moselle. The sloping flanks of the Rhine Valley nurtured the roots of yet more vines, while in France, along the Rhône and in Bordeaux and Burgundy, growers tended the vines that had started out as cuttings from Greece and Southern Italy. Old manuscripts and books contain many illuminated pages and paintings showing the peasants at work among the vines. In the background, usually, there stands a crenelated castle or rambling château where the vineyardist lived. But neither the lord of the manor nor his serfs lived too well. For them, life was often a daily scramble to get enough to eat, let alone to drink.

"Good wine was welcome," we are told, "inferior wine was tolerated; and almost any wine was preferable to none at all."

A writer of the period observed, though, that there was no shortage of wine in terms of physical volume from "thousands of vineyards" along the valleys of the Tiber, the Arno, the Po, the Guadalquivir, and other western European waters. We're left in doubt, however, about the quality of the wine. "Wine flowed along the

A small Romano-Syrian bronze figure from the second century A.D. of a minor deity of drink holding a shallow cup in his right hand. 2½" high. The Christian Brothers Collection.

rivers," our scribe noted, "and over the land and sea to console the toilers of Europe's fields, workshops, and counting rooms."

Ancient Viticulture

One of the great extravagances of speech about wine is that it makes itself, that man provides the ingredients and then stands back to let Nature take its course. Up to a point, that's true; and surely as we look back upon earlier winemaking, charity persuades us to excuse our forebears if, in the absence of the science that has enhanced today's wines, they enthused over products that would leave us cold. The solemn fact is that viticulture — the science of the vine — and enology — the science of winemaking — were not yet in being. The winegrowers of that period had no choice but to trust that Divine Providence would endow the grapes with ample natural sugar and other physical properties to bring about just the right result of fermentation. It was not until much later that Abraham Lincoln put the pious thought into words on the coin of the realm, but European vintners of the Middle Ages by their unflinching faith in the powers of soil, water, and sun could have inspired that motto: "In God We Trust."

Still, they weren't sitting on their hands. While putting the fate of the crop and the vintage in the hands of the Almighty, they adopted some innovations in the care of their wines that removed some of the guesswork. The wooden cask, the glass bottle, and the cork seem basic to us now, but they were long strides toward preservation and enhancement of the product — which, if exposed to the slightest currents of air, wouldn't last much beyond the fall crush.

Emerging Technology

It wasn't until the sixteenth century, when the Middle Ages had receded into the pages of history, that enologists adapted a known technique — the burning of sulphur — to the sterilization of their vats and casks; sulphur was useful, too, as an agent in arresting fermentation, and as a preservative during the aging process in wines.

Casks, those barrel-shaped products of the

cooper's art, had been around a long time but mainly as shipping containers to replace the older and destructible earthenware amphorae. H. Warner Allen in his *History of Wine* credits German vintners with discovering that the sturdy oak barrel also created a hospitable environment for the aging of wines. The further belief that large casks preserved wines better than small ones touched off a competition among coopers to make ever-larger barrels. The first Heidelberg tun, built in 1591, held thirty-three thousand gallons; the second, still on display in Heidelberg, was built in 1663 and holds forty-nine thousand gallons. Still, these giants were dwarfed by the Königstein Tun, which, according to Allen, held nearly a million gallons. More

As shown in this engraved map from an 1663 atlas, the Archdiocese of Trier covered much of Germany's wine country. Mr. and Mrs. Alfred Fromm Collection.

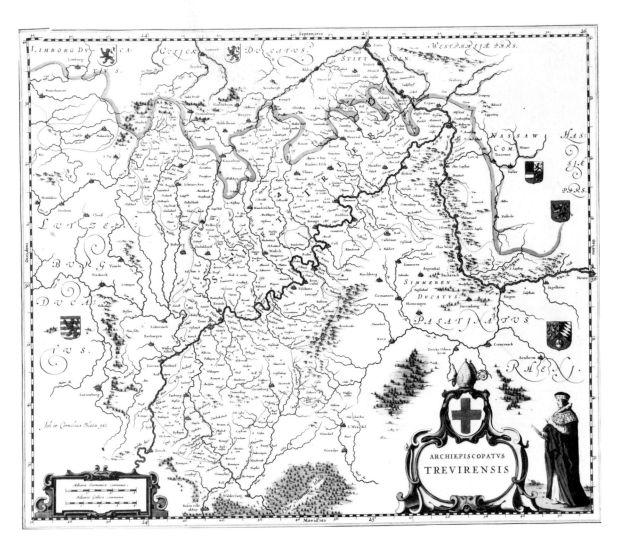

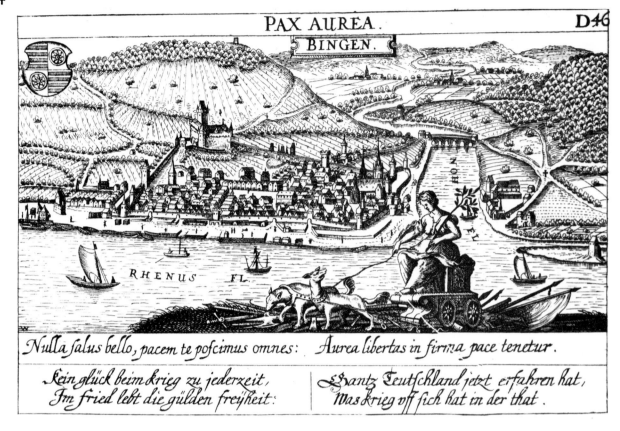

PAX AUREA.

BINGEN.

RHENUS FL.

D46

Nulla salus bello, pacem te poscimus omnes: *Aurea libertas in firma pace tenetur.*

Kein glück beim krieg zu jederzeit,
Im fried lebt die gülden freyheit:

Gantz Teutschland jetzt erfahren hat,
Was krieg uff sich hat in der that.

Bingen, one of the centers of German winegrowing on the Rhine River, was already surrounded by vineyards in the seventeenth century, as can be seen in this engraving from Daniel Meisner's Thesaurus Philo-Politicus, *1624–26.* The Christian Brothers Collection.

important than the competition for size was that at last man had found a way to age and preserve wine. Three centuries later, small wooden casks still play a vital role in aging, particularly of premium-quality red dinner wines.

With the emergence of cork as a stopper for the glass bottle, it became evident that wine — especially the reds — could acquire additional finish in the bottle. It was many years, however, before the right bottle shape evolved. The popular wine bottle was the "spike and globe" with its bulbous body rising to a spikelike neck. It was an aesthetic delight on the dinner table,

but useless for aging because it stood upright. Not until the eighteenth century did it dawn on vintners that, in a bottle that could lie on its side, the wine would keep the cork moist and minimize the risk of damaging oxidation through air seepage. Development of the cylindrical bottle, now standard, permitted the utilization of this natural phenomenon.

There is a temptation to suppose that the vine and the grape were the special possessions of the civilizations that flourished, roughly, on the perimeter of the Mediterranean — the northern coast of Africa, the Middle East, the uncounted

SCORTATIO ET VINUM ENERVANT COR HOMINIS.   A64

WERTHEIMER BURG.

Balnea, Vina, Venus juvenilia corpora sternunt. Exemplum tibi præbet in hoc audax Holofernes.

Der süsse Wein und Veneris spiel,
Verderben jung gesellen viel:

Darumb wiltu versichert sein,
So meyd die Lieb, die Nacht und Wein.

Wertheim Castle in the Franconia wine region of Central Germany is shown with its surrounding vineyards and accompanied by an allegory of Bacchus and Venus in this engraved illustration from Daniel Meisner's Thesaurus Philo-Politicus *of 1624–26. The Christian Brothers Collection.*

valleys of Italy, Greece, France, Germany, Spain, Portugal, even Britain. But five hundred years before Columbus discovered America and turned Europe's eyes to the West, the Viking Leif Ericsson lost his bearings and touched the shores of North America. He reported finding many grapevines along the coast, probably between Nova Scotia and Cape Cod. So abundant were the vines and their fruit that he dubbed the place *Vinland,* or Wineland, and took a load of grapes to Greenland with him. If the Norsemen ever experimented with the juice of the grapes, the fact was not recorded. It was clear, though, that the Eastern Hemisphere had no monopoly on the vine.

The Renaissance

Not all the ferment was in the wine. In Italy and spreading out from there to France and Germany, to Spain, to the Low Countries and England, and to all of Europe, there blossomed an intellectual and cultural awakening that left an indelible stamp on the fourteenth and fifteenth centuries and scarcely exhausted itself in the sixteenth. The Renaissance raised the curtain on a world stage that introduced a number of

BACHARACH & WERNERS KAPELLE

Glück und Glaß, wie bald bricht das.

BernCastel

MOSELLA. FLV.

Cum ridet Fortuna nimis, cave, rumpitur ultro, Cum splendent, facilè vitrea vasa crepant.

Ein Glaß clar und lieblich außsicht, Das Glück ist gläsern bricht auch bald,
Doch ist es schwach und leichtlich bricht. Drumb dasselbig in Ehren halt.

Opposite top
Named after Bacchus, Bacharach on the Rhine was one of the foremost German winegrowing and shipping centers. This view of Bacharach showing the Rhine in the background is a nineteenth-century steel engraving by Johann Richter after a drawing by Ludwig Lange. The Christian Brothers Collection.

Above
This nineteenth-century hand-colored steel engraving by Julius Umbach (after a drawing by Ludwig Rohbock) clearly shows the vineyards surrounding Hochheim on the River Main that produce some of the famous Rhine wines referred to as "Hock" in England, a bastardization of the city's name. The Christian Brothers Collection.

Opposite bottom
Berncastel on the Moselle River, where winegrowing dates back to the Romans, is shown in this seventeenth-century engraving, along with a pictorial representation of the German proverb: "Glass and luck are easily broken." The Christian Brothers Collection.

38

immortals: Copernicus, Galileo, Bacon, Michelangelo, the Borgias, Raphael, da Vinci, and later Newton and Leibnitz. These were the adventurers of the mind. There were also the seafarers, the explorers who didn't change the surface of the earth but did drastically refine man's understanding of it: Christopher Columbus, Henry Hudson, Sir Francis Drake, Sir Walter Raleigh, John Cabot, and many more.

Columbus opened the Caribbean in four voyages beginning in 1492. Twenty-seven years later, Hernán Cortés was at the gates of Mexico. Cortés discovered and destroyed the Mayan-Aztec civilization, and the extraordinary fact of the New World was laid bare. In a generation, the world had doubled in size.

The joyful vintage festival parade at Klosterneuburg celebrating the 1834 harvest is captured in this lithograph by Franz Wolf. Klosterneuburg is still a well-known wine-producing district and is high on the list of places to visit for the wine-thirsty tourists. The Christian Brothers Collection.

Das große Weinfass auf dem Königstein.

In this mid-seventeenth-century anonymous engraving of the great Heidelberg Tun, the German artist presents the tun commissioned by Elector Carl Ludwig in 1663. The second in a series of three, it was lavishly ornamented with bacchanalian scenes. Like its predecessor, which was a casualty of the Thirty Years' War, it became a victim of time and was replaced by a new tun, which still exists today. The Christian Brothers Collection.

Das Grosse Weinfass auf dem Königstein, *a hand-colored engraved illustration from an 1813 German magazine, shows only a frontal view of this gigantic tun with the Royal Saxonian coat-of-arms above the royal initials. Commissioned by the Polish Governor in 1725, the famous tun bore the following inscription:* "Welcome traveller, admire this monument, dedicated to festivity, by Frederick Augustus, King of Poland, Elector of Saxony, the father of his country, the Titus of the age, the delight of mankind. Therefore drink to the health of the sovereign, the country, the electoral family, and the Baron Kyaw, Governor of Konigstein; and if thou art able, according to the capacity of this tun, the most capacious of casks, drink to the prosperity of the whole universe — and so farewell." (Redding trans.) The Christian Brothers Collection.

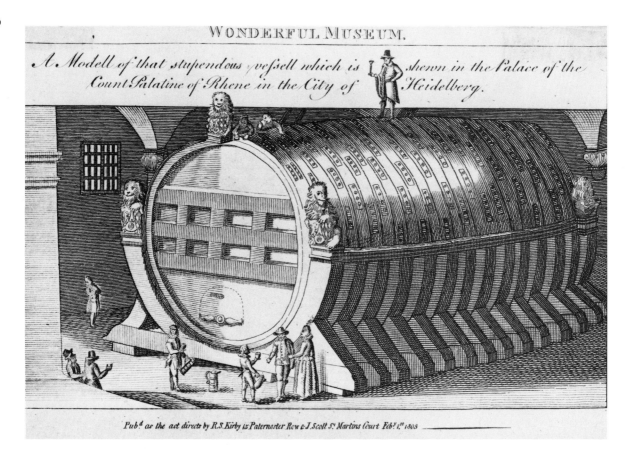

A Modell of that stupendous vessell which is shewn in the Palace of the Count Palatine of Rhene in the City of Heidelberg.

Pub.d as the act directs by R.S.Kirby 11 Paternoster Row & J.Scott St Martins Court Feby 1st 1803

To this newly discovered land, Cortés first brought wine from Spain, for table and sacramental use. He later sent home for vine cuttings to produce his own grapes and wine, for cargo space in the ships from Spain was too scarce to establish a maritime pipeline. Solemnly the conqueror decreed that vines be planted on every farm. Although the vineyards that sprang to life at Cortés' command were far from the first on this continent, they, rather than the wild vines Ericsson found in *Vinland*, were the forerunners of the vines that now feed most of the American wine market. We shall see in Chapter III why this occurred.

Colonial Failure

The distressing fact was that the grapes along the eastern coast, however abundant, produced disappointing wine. In 1616, Lord Delaware urged the cultivation of the vine in Virginia,

The great tun that may still be seen in the Königsaal, or Great Hall, of the Heidelberg Castle was constructed in 1751 by Jakob Engler the Younger for Elector Karl Theodor. The third of its kind in Heidelberg, it was only filled three times and the wine was pumped to the upper floors so that the servants did not have to continually return to the cellar for refills. Already a curiosity in 1803, it is the subject of this English engraving entitled: "WONDERFUL MUSEUM. A Modell of that stupendous vessell which is shown in the Palace of the Count Palatine of Rhene in the City of Heidelberg." The Christian Brothers Collection.

and in 1619, European vine dressers were dispatched to plant cuttings from their own vineyards on the Continent. The cuttings didn't root. Virginia authorities, accustomed to their nip of Madeira, or claret, offered incentives in the form of bounties and bonuses to anyone who could make the European vines grow or make a palatable wine from the native grapes. The effort was a dismal flop.

Governor Winthrop of the Massachusetts Bay Colony tried his hand at viticulture on an island in Boston Harbor around 1630. His plantings died. In Maine and Rhode Island, imported vines failed. The Dutch tried winemaking, and the Swedes, and William Penn. All failed. The wine-producing vine from Europe would not thrive and the abundant native grapes would not make good wine.

In viticultural terms, it was clear that the revolutionaries who took England's measure on the field of battle were inferior to their foe in

In the mid-nineteenth century, Nicholas Longworth first succeeded in producing good American wine from the native Catawba grapes that grew in the terraced, densely planted vineyards along the Ohio River, as is shown in this woodcut illustration from an 1866 pamphlet. The Christian Brothers Collection.

the vineyards. George Washington planted vines at Mount Vernon; nothing came of it. Thomas Jefferson imported vines from Europe and entrusted them to the soil of Monticello. They failed. He encouraged perseverance with American grapes, but it was notable that his own cellar was stocked with French wines.

Ultimately, Nicholas Longworth — a New Jersey horticulturist and great-grandfather of the man who became Speaker of the U.S. House of Representatives — bowed to the inevitable and transferred his vineyard experiments to the "frontier," Ohio. Even there, on the Ohio River near Cincinnati, the European vines he had imported by the thousands failed; but he achieved notable success in producing wines from the native Catawba and Isabella grapes. A gift of this wine to Henry Wadsworth Longfellow in 1854 inspired the lilting poem, "Catawba Wine," the first verse of which graces an early page of this book.

In the first half of the nineteenth century, California winegrowing first expanded northward along the coastal valleys; later, as transportation and water supplies became available, it entered the Central Valley. The Bella Vista Vineyard in Cordelia, Solano County, which was owned by John Votypks, is the subject of this two-tone lithograph from The San Francisco Illustrated Wasp *of September 29, 1877.* The Christian Brothers Collection.

Opposite
Irish immigrant vintner, James Concannon (left, with beard), brought this cider press from Maine to press grapes at his newly founded vineyard in Alameda County, California, in the late nineteenth century. Photo Courtesy Concannon Vineyards.

*Hillside vineyards were already well established in
the 1860s in California, as can be seen in this
photograph taken in the Santa Clara Valley area.*
Photo Courtesy Mirassou Vineyards.

44

1. KOHLER & FROHLING'S WINE-CELLAR, IN SONOMA COUNTY. 2. EDGE HILL VINEYARD, IN NAPA COUNTY. 3. MISSION SAN JOSÉ VINEYARD, IN ALAMEDA COUNTY.

CENTRAL CALIFORNIA.—FROM PHOTOGRAPHS BY TABER, OF SAN FRANCISCO.

Lurking Culprit

What those early American vineyardists did not know was that their problem lay not in the soil, certainly not in the quality of the rootstock they imported from Europe, and not entirely in the climatic extremes of the New England coast. The problem was instead entomological, a capricious root-louse with the florid name *Phylloxera*. For reasons still unknown, roots of the hardy wild vines of North America were immune to the pest while those nurtured in European soil fell easy prey to it. The nineteenth century was well along and civilization's most productive European vineyards infested and almost wiped out before the scourge was detected. How the viticulturists outfoxed the wily insect is a scientific cliffhanger that we will examine later in Chapter III.

His Hispanic Majesty's minions who approached this continent through Mexico and fanned out north and south had, oddly, no struggle with the root-louse. Cortés saw to it that the area of his conquest was assiduously vined, and when Jesuit missionaries moved into Baja California, they too displayed viticultural élan. But José Galvez, dispatched by Charles III in 1761

to clean up an administrative mess in Mexico, sent the Jesuits packing because, he alleged, they overstepped the parochial boundaries of their work and interfered with affairs of state.

The Jesuits were replaced by the pious "friars minor" in the steps of St. Francis of Assisi — the Franciscans whose stamp on California is still visible in the chain of twenty-one missions they established between 1769 and 1823. Now secularized and many of them restored as historic monuments to these architects of California's early culture, the missions were strung out from what is now San Diego to Sonoma, north of San Francisco.

The frail Majorcan, Fra Junípero Serra, pushed north from Baja California with its governor, Gaspar de Portola, under a dual assignment from Galvez to establish centers of civilization along the trail and to bring Christianity to the natives he encountered. The names of the missions that Serra and his successors founded in fifty-four years are redolent of the romance entwined in California's history: San Juan Capistrano, San Luis Rey, San Miguel, San Juan Bautista, Soledad, San Luis Obispo, San Carlos Borromeo, San Gabriel, and the "nameplate" mission at San Francisco, Misión de Nuestro Padre San Francisco de Assisi — the "Mission Dolores," in popular usage.

Mission Vineyards

Fra Serra and the friars who followed in his steps when he died in 1784 at San Carlos Borromeo, his ecclesiastical command post near the mouth of the Carmel River, had no choice but to become vintners. As Catholic priests, they had to celebrate Mass daily, and each repetition of the solemn service called for a few ounces of pure grape wine. Also, being Europeans with a cultivated taste for wine with meals, they knew they were in trouble if they waited for Galvez to supply them from Mexico. Accordingly, they set their vine cuttings in the ground around the missions as quickly as they planted wheat and corn. The vines flourished, the good padres satisfied their sacramental needs, and enough wine was left to take the rough edge

Opposite
A wood-engraved illustrated page from Frank Leslie's Illustrated Newspaper *of December 24, 1887, lauds the wine industry of Central California: 1. Charles Kohler and John Frohling produced good wine in Los Angeles beginning in 1854 and later established a vineyard and winery in Glen Ellen in Sonoma County in 1874. 2. Edge Hill Vineyard in Napa County. 3. Mission San José Vineyard, then owned by the brother of the famed Leland Stanford, U.S. senator, governor of California, and founder of Stanford University, is now owned by the Weibel family.* The Christian Brothers Collection.

off their frugal noonday dinner and evening supper.

There is no evidence that the mission wines earned any gold medals for quality, but it's noteworthy that California vintners today, pressed for more and more suitable vineyard acreage, are retreating two hundred years into the pages of history to cultivate some of the very soil that nourished the friars' vines. This is conspicuously true in San Benito and Monterey counties, where some leading growers have undertaken extensive plantings.

We don't have to dig very deeply into historical records to discover that the padres were "father" to more than the spiritual need of early Californians — the wagon-train pioneers, the adventurous sailing-ship passengers who came 'round the Horn, and His Majesty's grandees who had been given ranchos so large that they couldn't see from one end to the other. However the settlers may have admired the friars for their piety and good works, they reserved their warmest affection for the Franciscans' way with a grape.

At the Misión de San Francisco Solano in Sonoma, Padre José Altimira got his vines into the ground within a year after he established the mission in 1823. He would enjoy the fruit of his labor only a few years, for in 1833 the Mexican Government, having wriggled free from Spain, set about dividing the mission lands among settlers, and the missions were inactivated, some even closed. Fra Altimira's vineyards were not desolated, however; instead they were taken over by General Mariano Vallejo, Mexico's military commandant at Sonoma. The valleys around Sonoma and neighboring Napa County remain to this day the cradle of some of California's loveliest wines.

In 1831 the French cooper, Jean Louis Vignes, carrying vines from his native Bordeaux, arrived in Los Angeles (served by the San Gabriel Mission) and planted 104 acres on the site of what is now the Union Railroad Station. Vignes is said to have become the most important producer of wine on the Pacific Coast. A settler from Massachusetts, Joseph Chapman, learned primitive viticulture and enology from the padres at San Gabriel, and produced wines as early as 1827. And, there's a record of a Kentucky trapper, William Wolfskill, who became a landed proprietor and vintner in Los Angeles, while a relative, John Wolfskill, duplicated his success in Napa County, far to the north.

For sheer splendor and dash, however, and for what today would be called charisma by some, *chutzpa* by others, there was never a match for the Magyar revolutionist, "Count" Agoston Haraszthy de Mokesa, who endured his exile from Hungary in breathless pursuit of success in commerce, in politics, in trade, in intrigue — and in viticulture. In 1850, fresh from the Santa Fe Trail, he planted vineyards in San Diego. Moving north later as a member of the state legislature, he planted vines near Mission Dolores in San Francisco, and finally settled on the historic Buena Vista ranch near Sonoma. The Buena Vista, having lain dormant for many years, is again growing and crushing varietal grapes. But Haraszthy? He didn't choose his fate, of course, but it was characteristic. Traveling in Nicaragua, he fell into a stream and was eaten by crocodiles.

Opposite
This charming and amusing late-nineteenth-century poster bears the following note: "The above sketch is intended to illustrate the value of Irrigated land in comparison with land subject to drought or excessive rain, also the profit of Wine Growing over wheat and stock raising; but it is NOT intended to represent the present appearance of the Easterby Rancho. It would do very well, however, for a view of the Eisen Vineyard which adjoins this property — THE BEST VINEYARD LAND IN CALIFORNIA." Special Collections, University of California, Davis.

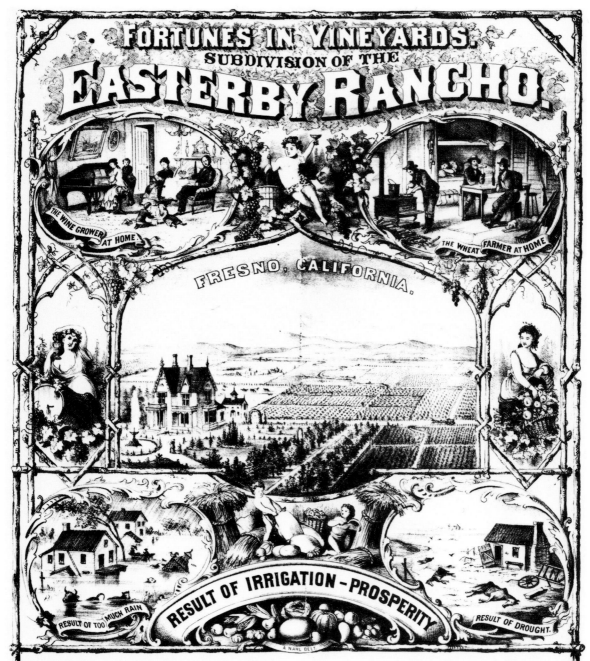

Willard Cox · Napa Valley · *The Novitiate and Vineyards at Mont La Salle*

From such primitive beginnings grew one of the sturdy foundations of California's agricultural economy. Although the Haraszthys, the Chapmans, and the Wolfskills have left the scene, there are now perhaps a hundred able and dedicated vintners and a thousand grape growers for each of the pioneers — among them Wente, Concannon, Captain Gustave Niebaum, Paul Masson, Mirassou, and such giant producers as the Gallo brothers, Italian Swiss Colony, and other firms. Many of those pioneer names remain viable today, augmented by the dedication of other companies and individuals. Brother Timothy, F.S.C., the cellar-master for Mont La Salle

Located in the foothills of the Napa Valley in California, Mont La Salle is the location of The Christian Brothers novitiate and winery. In 1932 The Brothers moved to this beautiful site from Martinez and named their new headquarters after the order's founder, Saint Jean Baptiste de la Salle. The novitiate and vineyards are the subject of this contemporary pencil drawing by Willard Cox. The Christian Brothers Collection.

Vineyards, the wine-producing arm of The Brothers of the Christian Schools, is but one example of the latter.*

Though the central interest of The Christian Brothers has always been teaching (there are currently eleven thousand of them staffing some thirteen hundred schools around the world), they became growers nearly a century ago, almost by accident. In 1879, The Brothers leased property to use as a novitiate near the small California town of Martinez and found a small vineyard awaiting them. They encouraged the vines, and, by 1882, made and sold a little sacramental wine, and lo!—there was some financial support for their schools. In 1931, The Brothers moved the novitiate and winery to larger quarters in the Napa Valley. This provided them with more extensive vineyards and gave them a solid base on which to build an inventory of fine wines. Thus, they were prepared for the fledgling public market that opened up after the repeal of Prohibition. At an early stage, The Brothers realized that Napa's climate and soil were best suited to the production of fine premium table wines, a fact that has made the Valley America's foremost premium wine district.

In 1935 Brother Timothy, who was teaching in The Christian Brothers schools, was drafted to help in the vineyard and in the winery. Upon the death of his predecessor, he became chief cellarmaster. Today, Brother Timothy is a prominent figure among the vintners of California — particularly of the Napa Valley — and must be counted among the most knowledgeable men in the industry. In the fashion of a Junípero Serra or a José Altimira, though, he manages to combine his vocation with his avocation in the prayer he breathes when invited to ask the blessing at meals:

"Almighty God, You who made the universe so large that man has never been able to measure it although he can go to the moon and back; you are the same God who created microscopic yeast cells too small for man to see; and you placed them on the skins of grapes so that the merest squeezing of the fruit begins fermentation and gives us wine: We ask you, O God, to bless us and the wines and foods we are about to enjoy."

As they say in prayers, So be it. . . .

---

* Throughout this volume, you will find special emphasis given to the winery operations of The Christian Brothers, whose artworks collection is the source of many of the accompanying illustrations. The authors, while recognizing that there are both differences and similarities among the world's thousands of wine producers, have chosen to use the winery operations of The Brothers as representative of much that is good in the making and marketing of premium wine.

50

*Fortuna pours out the horn of plenty before Hercules
in this etching done in 1617 by Jacob de Gheyn III.
The Christian Brothers Collection.*

2 *"I'm Drinking Stars!"*

It is not only for conviviality that man has put wine on a pedestal. If his need had been merely for a lift, a surge of exaltation and well-being, over the ages he could have turned to beer; and in more recent days to a choice of distilled spirits, surely a more direct road to exhilaration.

Man has in fact found all of these, wine included, to be useful adjuncts to his social life. But among all the beverages, he has elevated wine alone to a role of sublime dignity in his spiritual life. This was true not only of Jew and Christian in what, as history is measured, we may call "recent" times but also of much earlier civilizations. With a few notable exceptions of peoples that regarded the grape and its product dubiously, mankind has for centuries looked upon wine as a boon to both body and spirit.

Nowhere is this more evident than in the mythology of ancient Greece, which became the foundation, the underpinnings, of a culture that was destined to envelop much of the human race. Lacking any rational concept for the mystery of Creation, the ancient Greek had to invent one. His invention was the colony of supernatural beings that inhabited the ethereal Mount Olympus — his gods. Until Jews of prophetic vision fixed upon Yahweh as the God of all Creation, the mighty gods of Greek mythology were the ruling divinities.

The Dionysian Cult

A considerable body of classical sculpture, art, literature, and drama was built up around the god Dionysus, the deity responsible for the health of the vine, the abundance of the harvest, and the fermentation of the juices tramped out of the grapes. It is impossible to establish precisely when Dionysus entered the stream of consciousness of his followers — an element of vagueness that is characteristic of all the mythological heroes. Even his most lucid biographer, Euripides, failed to dispel the mist clouding the knowledge of when the Dionysian cult was born. This much we know: A year after Euripides, the dramatic poet whose works lent power and grace to the theater in Athens, died in 406 B.C. in Macedonia at the age of seventy-five, his play, *The Bacchae*, dramatizing an event in the adult years of Dionysus, was given its first production. This would establish the fifth century B.C. as the latest period for the origin of the cult. Supporting this is the generally accepted understanding that the earliest attempt to unravel the meaning of classical myths was that of Cyrenaic philosopher Euhemerus around the fourth century B.C.

Illustrations in this book and additional exhibits in The Wine Museum of San Francisco represent no more than a sampling of the cultural works linking Dionysus with wine. So firm was the bond of the people to the god that the devotion to him jumped national boundaries to take fresh root in the Roman Empire, where Dionysus/Bacchus was identified as Liber.*

In 186 B.C., the Roman Senate, alarmed over the hysteria that gripped participants in the Bacchanalia, the transplanted rites of the Dionysian festival, legislated the celebrations out of existence under penalty of severe punishment. A deity who could evoke such passionate response from his followers, arouse such fear in the lawgivers, and inspire artists of pen, brush, and chisel to preserve his image down the centuries, deserves inspection in a book concerned with wine, his special province.

Legend of a God

Dionysus was said to be the youngest of the gods on Mount Olympus and the only one to have a mortal parent. The legend of his origin, which seems to gather embellishment at each telling, is that his father was Zeus, the supreme god of Greek religion, and his mother the mortal Semele, daughter of Cadmus.

Zeus in his romance made no secret of his divinity but wooed the maiden in his mortal

* The Romans renamed all the Olympian gods: Zeus became Jupiter, sometimes Jove, in Rome; Hermes, Mercury; Hephaestus, Vulcan; Aphrodite, Venus; Hera, Juno; Poseidon, Neptune.

In this delightful eighteenth-century French parcel-gilt bronze statuette, the artist chose to depict Bacchus as a playful child squeezing grapes into a cup. At his feet are a tambourine and a thyrsus staff, objects used in the bacchantic dances of the Maenads. 8" high. The Christian Brothers Collection.

Opposite
This Sèvres French bisque porcelain figure group represents the triumph of Bacchus. Bacchus is being offered grapes and wine by two maenads, while three children, a leopard, and implements of hunting and the arts surround the group. After a model by Hugues Taraval, it is marked 1773. 13½" high.
The Christian Brothers Collection.

Gabriel Müller's engraving dated 1771, after
Hendrik Goltzius, depicts Bacchus as the god of
wine. Draped in grapes and holding aloft a cup of
wine, the oval-framed image is flanked by satyrs'
masks and contemporary wineglasses. The Christian
Brothers Collection.

In a matching engraving, also by Gabriel Müller and
dated 1771, Ceres is represented as the goddess of
harvest. She holds the mystic basket filled with the
fruits of the harvest and her image is framed by
her attributes. The Christian Brothers Collection.

guise. Goaded by a jealous rival for the god's attentions, the pregnant Semele insisted that Zeus prove his divinity by appearing before her in his Olympian majesty. He did so reluctantly, and the divine fire of his terrible thunderbolts reduced Semele to ashes. Zeus rescued the fetus from her womb and inserted it in his own thigh for the remaining gestation period. When the child Dionysus was born, so the legend goes, he was removed from a fold of flesh in his father's leg.

A minor god, Silenus, became Dionysus' tutor and lifelong companion. And though Silenus in the literature of mythology is portrayed as a kindly lush, he is also credited with teaching his young charge that wine is not an unmixed blessing; that wine in excess may lead to weakness and brutality, while in moderation it promotes freedom and buoyancy. This helps to explain why Dionysus, in the tradition that comes down through the ages, personifies both the positive and the negative aspects of wine. On the one hand, his physical beauty as a youth symbolizes the beneficial values in wine; on the other, the proscribed three-day orgies known in Italy as Bacchanalia reduced the participating maenads, satyrs, and nymphs of the forest to the level of beasts.

It was incumbent on the gods to win acceptance of their divinity among mortals before they could ascend Mount Olympus and take the places reserved for the twelve Olympian deities. Much of the literature is concerned with Dionysus' struggles to convince even his own relatives that he was indeed a god. At the royal palace at Thebes, Dionysus exhorted his cousin Pentheus, the king, to acknowledge his divinity. Failing, he imposed a frightful penalty on his cousin: Pentheus was driven mad and ripped to pieces by his own mother, who mistook him for a lion. The angry god inflicted the same madness on the daughters of King Proetus of Argos, although they were later cured.

A Greedy King

Dionysus is pictured in more benevolent posture in the familiar legend of King Midas of

In this lovely bistre pen drawing by the early-eighteenth-century Spanish artist Lucas de Valdés, Bacchus is shown as a young man raising a glass of wine. The Christian Brothers Collection.

In this early-nineteenth-century etching and aquatint
by Frederick Christian Lewis after a drawing by
Nicolas Poussin, three satyrs are shown playing with
a goatskin flask. The Christian Brothers Collection.

Opposite
In this engraving dated 1596 by Jean Saenredam, the
artist combines an ancient myth with contemporary
images. A classical Bacchus is being venerated
by sixteenth-century individuals. The Christian
Brothers Collection.

HL Goltzius.
Santredam sculp.

Bacche pater, prono prostrati corpore cuncti,   Dona, quibus mæror tristis, luctusq; recedit,
Suppliciter petimus, nobis tua dona secundes.   Nostraq; sollicitis relevantus pectora curis.

C. Schonæus.

Opposite
A late-nineteenth-century Italian representation of a satyr as a shepherd offering grapes. His shoulders draped with a goatskin, he stands between a tree stump and a basket with a lamb perched on it. This patinated bronze statuette is signed "Chiurozzi, Napoli." 28" high. The Christian Brothers Collection.

This late-eighteenth-century terra-cotta sculptural group in the manner of Clodion shows a satyr playfully offering a grape to a nude maenad as she embraces him. In the forefront are a syrinx and a thyrsus, dancing implements of the maenad. 13½" high. The Christian Brothers Collection.

Phrygia. In that tale, the tipsy tutor, Silenus, wandered off and was lost in Phrygia, while he and his charge were en route back to Greece from India. Taken to the king, Silenus entertained him with tales of adventure. In gratitude Midas restored the wanderer to Dionysus, who thereupon offered the king any reward that lay in his divine power. Every schoolboy knows

In this early-seventeenth-century interpretation, Bacchus is shown presenting a grape and accompanied by three bacchantic children; etching in roundel attributed to Cornelis Schut. The Christian Brothers Collection.

what the greedy king coveted most. So Midas got his wish, but obtained the god's release from it when even all food and wine turned to gold at his touch. At length the son of Zeus and Semele won the acceptance he sought and took his place on Olympus.

Where does myth end and reality begin? The question is asked again and again. One rational view of Dionysus is expressed in *The New Century Classical Handbook*, published in 1962 by Appleton-Century-Crofts. The editors note that Dionysus was the god of the vine, of fertility, and of joyous life; the god of hospitality and of peace; and was associated with Apollo and the Muses as a god of poets and musicians. The book recalls that Dionysus was honored

Pablo Picasso shows satyrs joyously dancing while making music with trumpets and cymbals in this modern interpretation of a bacchanal. The lithograph is dated "Sunday, May 24, 1957" in the stone. The Christian Brothers Collection.

Si renuunt latices dulces intrare, Sodales
Vectibus & fidibus præcipitentur ii. C.

Sam. Bottschilt, inv. et fectt.

This late-seventeenth-century etching by Samuel
Bottschild, which depicts a bacchanal with satyrs
and maenads, is in the form of a ceiling-vault design.
The Christian Brothers Collection.

Charles Nicolas Cochin in this etching dated 1745
and entitled Feste en l'honneur de Bacchus *(after a*
design by Alexandre Denis de Niert, Marquis de
Gambais) shows the exuberance of a bacchantic
celebration. The festivities, led by Silenus, are being
held around a statue of Bacchus, of which only the
lower portion and pedestal are visible. The Christian
Brothers Collection.

In this scene from the wanderings of Bacchus by the mid-seventeenth-century artist Pierre Brebiette, Diana and Minerva are shown fleeing upon the arrival of Bacchus and his entourage who are led by an elephant festooned with grapevines, carrying cupids and a sleeping leopard on his back. The Christian Brothers Collection.

with periodic multiple festivals known as the Dionysia, among them the notable Greater Dionysia, a five-day celebration in the spring when commerce was halted, prisoners freed, and the works of poets and musicians were performed in open-air theaters.

"Even to observe them was an act of worship," says *The New Century*. "The works the poets and musicians wrote for the Greater Dionysia were the foundation, and ultimately the whole magnificent structure, of Greek drama. The dithyramb, the form used by the poets, was invented . . . in honor of Dionysus."

Does it matter, then, whether the "twice-born" god who rose to Olympus was a creature of fantasy — or something else?

L'Alliance de Bacchus et de Venus *is an eighteenth-century engraving by Jacque Philippe le Bas after Noel-Nicolas Coypel.* The Christian Brothers Collection.

An enchanting smile illuminates the face of a young bacchant, or follower of Dionysus, in this patinated bronze bust by the nineteenth-century French sculptor, Jean Baptiste Carpeaux. 23″ high.
The Christian Brothers Collection.

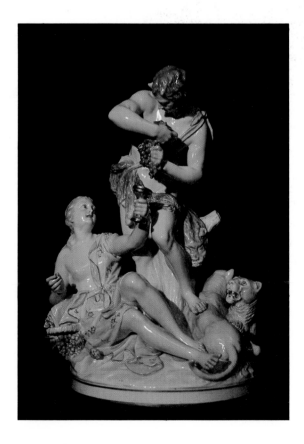

A satyr leans on a pair of panthers while squeezing grapes into the goblet of a recumbent nymph, in this delicate polychromed porcelain figure made by a Berlin manufacturer, about 1825. 9½″ high.
The Christian Brothers Collection.

3.6.56.

Pablo Picasso's strikingly colorful lithograph of a faun and sailor, dated June 3, 1956, served as the cover illustration for the Catalogue of Galerie 65 at Cannes. *Although a modern print, the trumpet-blowing faun harks back to the musical, boisterous bacchanalian activities depicted in earlier literature and art.* The Christian Brothers Collection.

Opposite
Bacchus is shown as an old man asleep in front of a barrel while mischievous children play around him in this sixteenth-century German woodcut by Hans Baldung. The child on the left holds a typical cylindrical drinking glass of the time. The Christian Brothers Collection.

A sixteenth-century Flemish artist presents Bacchus and Ceres feasting with companions in this brown ink, pen, and wash drawing. The Christian Brothers Collection.

Opposite
A senior Bacchus embraces a nymph in this color lithograph by Hans Erni, a twentieth-century Swiss artist. The Christian Brothers Collection.

68

The faithful, drunken tutor of Bacchus, Silenus, is shown in the company of frolicking satyrs in this engraving dated 1642 by the Flemish artist Pieter Soutman, after a painting by Peter Paul Rubens. The Christian Brothers Collection.

Opposite
The drunken Silenus, his body draped with a deerskin and a goatskin bag hanging from his shoulder, jovially raises a cup in his left hand while his right holds a lyre of ram's horns. This early twentieth-century bronze statuette is by Carl Brose, a German who was active in Dresden. 14½" high. The Christian Brothers Collection.

Silenum Patrem, Bacchi nutritium, Ventricosum temulentum, inter Satyras libidines spumantem, tabella hac exhibet.

In this etching, dated 1628, by José de Ribera, the Spanish artist represents Silenus as a pot-bellied old man holding aloft a conch-shell cup into which a satyr pours wine from a goatskin flask. Another satyr crowns him with grapevines while others look on. His braying ass looks upon the scene from the upper right corner, while in the lower left the panpipe of Silenus lies forgotten. The Christian Brothers Collection.

Canaan's "Firstripe" Grapes

The first Hebrew child to thrill at the exploits of Noah in his wondrous houseboat learned that the pious man, at the end of his hegira of forty days and forty nights, planted a vineyard, drank of the wine it produced, and eased into deep slumber — as have other sons of Adam in the years since that detail was recorded in the Book of Genesis. Moses, we are told in the Book of Numbers, sent Joshua and Caleb, in a reconnaissance party representing all Twelve Tribes of Israel, into Canaan to assess the prospect for the good life in the Promised Land, and instructed them to bring back to him in Egypt samples of any fruit they found. After forty days the advance party returned with pome-

This late-nineteenth-century silver goblet with engraved decoration bears a Hebrew inscription indicating that it was made as a Kiddush *cup for the celebration of the Jewish Passover.* The Christian Brothers Collection.

granates and figs, and with two of them shouldering a pole from which hung an enormous single cluster of "firstripe" grapes. Much, much later the festive wedding at Cana took place, where Jesus, at the behest of his mother, eased the host's embarrassment upon running out of wine by performing his first public miracle, changing water into wine.

While never countenancing immoderate use of wine, the Bible is replete with evidence that it was a staple of life support among our forebears. The Samaritan of Christ's parable, who "proved himself neighbor" to the Jew who was mugged on his way from Jerusalem to Jericho, had a little wine with him to restore the victim. The Psalmist rejoiced in "wine that maketh glad the heart of man." In Ecclesiastes we are counseled to "Go thy way, eat thy bread with joy and drink thy wine with a merry heart for God accepteth thy works." And Solomon sang: "Let us get up early to the vineyards; let us see if the vine flourish, whether the tender grapes appear . . . and there I will give thee my loves."

Yet, none of these paeans to the vine, its fruit, and its product could match the ineffable dignity that Jesus conferred upon wine at that final supper with his closest friends. He blessed the wine as he had blessed the bread and urged his companions to drink and eat, for these were now become the blood he was to shed and the body he was to surrender on Mount Calvary as the supreme act of love for all mankind. The bread and wine, as visible recreations of the eucharistic sacrament, have survived schism and reform, division, and apostasy for two thousand years in Christian worship. And, as noted in the preceding chapter, the sacramental injunction — "Do this in memory of me" — not only obliged the Christian missionaries to plant vines as and where they preached, it also accounted for the leap of European wine grapes to the New World.

Jewish Ritual

Neither Jew nor Christian, while embracing wine in his particular ceremonial rites, made it an object of worship as did the early Greeks

Aesop's Fable of the Fox and the Grapes: *A Fox,
very hungry, chanced to come into a Vineyard,
where there hung many bunches of charming ripe
grapes; but nailed up to a trellis so high, that he
leaped till he quite tired himself without being able
to reach one of them. At Last, "Let who will take
them!" says he; "they are but green and sour; so I
will even let them alone."*

*Oscar Kokoschka interprets the fable of "The Fox
and the Grapes" in this color lithograph of the mid-
twentieth century.* The Christian Brothers
Collection.

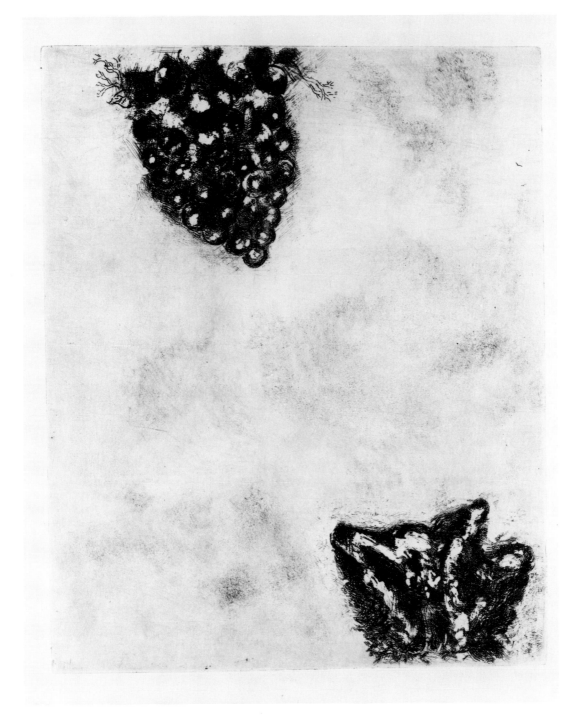

Aquatint etching by Marc Chagall from the illustrations of the Fables *by Jean de La Fontaine executed from 1927 to 1930, representing* "The Fox and the Grapes." Mr. and Mrs. Alfred Fromm Collection.

and often the Romans. The Jews laid the ecclesiastical foundations for the incorporation of wine into religious ritual; and the Jews who established the Christian faith made certain that the wine ritual was not lost in the new doctrine they preached.

The compilers of the Talmud considered well the voices of the prophets and concluded that moderation in drinking is better than total abstinence, that wine is often a sound medicine "and there is no gladness without it." In most joyous celebrations, such as a Bar Mitzvah, wine is an integral part of the feast. And at the beginning of each Sabbath, after the candles are blessed and lighted in every synagogue and in many Jewish homes, the wine is poured and blessed with song, following which each worshiper sips from his cup. For wine, in the Jewish tradition, is the symbol of joy.

Islamic Abstinence

While Europe struggled through the fervid years in search of God and nationality during the period that Christianity held western man together in a spiritual bond, a man widely regarded as the most influential person of the Middle Ages was born in far-off Arabia — the prophet, Muhammad. Born in Mecca in 570, Muhammad was a scion of the ruling clan, and his first years, now surrounded by fable, are misty. Muhammad in his forties immersed himself in religion, meditation, fasting, and prayer, and emerged after a series of visions as the messenger and true prophet of Allah, whom he proclaimed to be the one and only God.

A man of extraordinary faith, strength, and intelligence, Muhammad was able not only to establish the creed of Islam but also to unite the nomadic tribes of the desert into a nation and a religious force that still thrives. It is commonly thought that the *Koran* of Islam proscribes alcohol. In effect it does, but in an equivocal manner — that is, by observing that the sinful consequences of wine outweigh the beneficial uses. When the faithful Muslim goes to his eternal reward, however, he has the *Koran's* promise that in Paradise he will drink wine from gold and silver cups, have rivers of milk and honey, and deck himself in silken garments adorned with precious stones.

It is an oddity of Islam that one of its most noted practitioners, Omar Khayyam, is responsible for the oft-quoted line from the *Rubáiyát*, "A Jug of Wine, a Loaf of Bread — and Thou." Less well known is his mischievous "I wonder what the vintners buy, One-half so precious as the stuff they sell."

Thus, while the vine flourished in Europe, it withered in Islam. In other countries — India, China, Japan — it was never regarded as a friend. Even though China and Japan had native grape varieties and were leaders and innovators in horticulture, for the most part, they regarded the grapevine as a fruit and ornamental plant, and grape wine never became popular. Still, in the eighth century, the Chinese poet Li Po penned the rhythmic lines:

> "What a pleasure it is, with a cask of sweet wine
> And singing girls beside me,
> To drift hither and thither with the waves. . . ."

The great subcontinent of India was also content to ignore wine, although many parts of the country, particularly the northern slopes, would have been hospitable to the vine.

Opposite
Carved lindenwood Austrian barrelhead with Saint Anne teaching the young Virgin Mary within a frame of grapevines; signed "A.St." and dated 1770 on lower riband. 19" by 13½" oval. The Christian Brothers Collection.

A tall Bavarian Stangenglas *dated 1700 bears various quotations from the Bible and shows Christ blessing a penitent. 10-1/8" high.* Franz Sichel Glass Collection.

This gilt silver chalice is a beautiful example of the art of mid-nineteenth-century French silversmiths. On the cup are images of Christ, the Virgin Mary, and Joseph framed within rococo cartouches and the symbols of the Eucharist — grapes and wheat. Bulrushes, the symbol of the multitudes, grace the baluster stem; while on the tripartite foot appear the Holy Cross, the Lamb of God, and Flaming Hearts again topped by grapes. 11¼" high. The Christian Brothers Collection.

The drunkenness of Lot and the destruction of the cities of Sodom and Gomorrah (Genesis 19) are depicted in this mid-sixteenth-century woodcut attributed to Jost Amman. The Christian Brothers Collection.

Joshua and Caleb: ". . . and Moses sent them to spy out the land of Canaan and sait unto them, Get thou up this way southward, and go up into the mountain: And see the land, what it is; and the people that dwelleth therein. . . . And be ye of good courage, and bring of the fruit of the land. Now the time was of the firstripe grapes. So they went up, and searched the land from the wilderness of Zin unto Rehob. . . . and they ascended by the south. . . . and they came unto the brook of Eshcol, and cut down from thence a branch with one cluster of grapes, and they bare it between two upon a staff. . . .

"And they told him (Moses) and said, We came unto the land whither thou sentest us, and surely it floweth with milk and honey, and this is the fruit of it. . . ." Numbers 13:17–24

This early-sixteenth-century Dutch or Low German misericord is of oak wood and has a carved relief design of Joshua and Caleb carrying the large grape from Canaan; 9½" × 11½" × 6". The Christian Brothers Collection.

Duo viri portauerunt Botrum de terra pmissionis
in desertum. Numeri · xiij · c ·
Iosue vnd caleph die zwen iuden trůgen den weyntrauben auß dem gelobten land.

Respondit filius ecce ego mitto me · quia sum patr̄
Vade inquit pater cum hominib̄ couersare ibi · Et
pacienter sustine quicquid aplicatū fuerit tibi. Misus igitur filius dei viui conuersatus est in iudea · Et
nō peperunt ei · quia viliter interfectus est ab ea ·
Secūda figura.
Isto insinuauit xpistus i quadam parabola. Quā
pdicando iudeis tanquam figurā ppofuit de vinea
Homo quidam plantauit vineam z eam circumsepiuit · Extruens in ea turrim z torcular · colonis commisit. Tempe fructuum misit seruos suos qui fructus
exigebant · Quos illi apprehendentes cedebant z inficiebant. Quod audiens dominus misit alios suos
plures prioribus. Quibus illi fecerunt sicut fecerant
anterioribus. Ad vltimum autem misit eis vnicū
filium suum. Si forte verentur occidere illum. Quē
coloni apprehendentes de vinea eiecerunt · Et atrocr̄

Page from fifteenth-century German manuscript depicting Joshua and Caleb carrying the large bunch of grapes from Canaan; woodcut by Anton Sorg. The Christian Brothers Collection.

Exploratores terræ Canaan. Num. xiij.

Auffspeher des landes Canaan.
Num. xiij.

Exploratores Terra Canaan, Joshua and Caleb carrying the large bunch of grapes from Canaan. Early-sixteenth-century woodcut by Hans Sebald Beham. The Christian Brothers Collection.

Joshua and Caleb are depicted carrying the large grape from Canaan on these eighteenth-century Dutch blue-and-white fayence tiles; 17½" × 12" in frame. The Christian Brothers Collection.

This early-sixteenth-century brass pan or Blutschüssel was used to collect the blood in bloodletting, an especially popular medical practice of the time. Gothic lettering is embossed around the edges and the central relief of Joshua and Caleb carrying a large grape cluster is symbolic of the affinity between blood and wine. 12" in diameter. Mr. and Mrs. Alfred Fromm Collection.

*This eighteenth-century Austrian polychromed
statue shows Saint Urban holding a missal topped
with a grape cluster in his left hand, while his right
clutches a bishop's crozier. 29½" high.*
The Christian Brothers Collection.

Opposite
Angels Toiling in the Lord's Vineyard, *an early-
sixteenth-century woodcut book illustration by an
anonymous South German artist.* The Christian
Brothers Collection.

*Saint Geneviève's position as patroness of French
wine growers, and her contribution to the building
of the church of St. Denis in Paris, are both sym-
bolized in this carved lindenwood statue from
eastern France, dated about 1460. In her right hand,
she tenderly holds a grape cluster, while her left
clutches a model of the church. 39¾" high.*
The Christian Brothers Collection.

The biblical quotation, The Branch Cannot Bear Fruit Except it Abide in the Vine *(John 15:4), is illustrated in this hand-colored lithograph by Currier & Ives, New York, 1872.* The Christian Brothers Collection.

"And the third day there was a marriage in Cana of Galilee; . . . And when they wanted wine, . . . there were set there six water-pots of stone, . . . Jesus saith unto them, Fill the waterpots with water. And they filled them up to the brim. And he saith unto them, Draw out now, and bear unto the governor of the feast. And they bare it. When the ruler of the feast had tasted the water that was made wine, and knew not whence it was. . . ." John 2:1–9

The Wedding at Cana; line engraving by Giovanni Volpato dated 1772, after a painting by Jacopo Tintoretto in the sacristy of Santa Maria della Salute in Venice. The Christian Brothers Collection.

82

Benevolent Patron

Before concluding this account of the role that wine has played in the religions of the world, it's pleasant to recall some of the tales that have been woven about the relationship. Saint Geneviève, patron saint of Paris, is said to have bestowed her smile in a most gracious manner on the efforts of the faithful when, in 1133, they responded to the call of the Benedictine Abbot Suger to build a fitting church in Paris in honor of Saint Denîs, patron of France. Masons, glassmakers, stonecutters, sculptors, carpenters, laborers, goldsmiths, and draftsmen assembled to build the church where the mortal remains of France's kings would be laid to rest. To speed their labors and to hold their interest, the kindly Geneviève, we are told, saw to it that the workers were supplied with wine from an ever-gushing well. It may be noted that she did not cast her bread on still waters; for her saintly cooperation, she was acclaimed the patron saint of wine growers.

German winegrowers have their own patron in Saint Urban, and at one time took solemn note of the weather on his feast day. If it was sunny, that augured well for the grape crop; but if it rained, that spelled trouble, and the unhappy farmers often retaliated by dunking the statue of Saint Urban in a watering trough. Today he is spared this indignity, and his feast day is an occasion for distribution of a "Saint Urban gift" — bottles of wine — among the poor.

Not only through its foreign missions but in its established bases as well, the church took a hand in the development of wine. Gifts of vineyards by nobles enriched several religious orders, both materially and spiritually. It was a Benedictine monk, Dom Pérignon, who produced the first sparkling Champagne in the cellars of the Abbey of Hautvillers, France, sometime before 1715. In so doing, he left us two priceless legacies. One was the effervescent wine itself. The second was his delighted cry when he tasted the first sip: "Come quickly! I'm drinking stars!"

Generations of admirers have responded: "Alleluia!"

"Now it came to pass in the days of Ahasuerus . . . the king made a feast unto all the people that were present in Shushan the palace, both unto great and small, seven days, in the court of the garden of the king's palace. . . .

"And they gave them drink in vessels of gold, (the vessels being diverse one from another,) and royal wine in abundance, according to every man's pleasure. . . ." Book of Esther 1:1–7

Opposite
Page from early-sixteenth-century Nuremberg Bible depicting the banquet of King Ahasuerus, woodcut attributed to Hans Baldung. The Christian Brothers Collection.

¶ Der dryt teil diser hy stori ist die aller genad reichoste gesondmach ung/Wan als jetz das einhorn gefange ward jn der schoß der junck frawe/der son gotes jn dem junckfrölichen liß ward das getöt zu der zeit des leiden cristi jhe su/Vnd dan die wonden menschlicher natur mit dem plůt des einhorns besprentzt christi Jhesu/wurden alle menschen widerumb ge sond von jeren tötlichen schaden. ¶Wie dan geschriben stat Appoca.j. Qui dilexit. Der vns lieb gehept het auch von ewikeit/vnnd vns gewaschen jn seinem plůt von vnseren sünden/vnd vns gemacht das reich der hy mel/vnd priester got vnserem vater Amen.

Von der menschwerdong gotes als die gefiguriert ist jn dem buch hester.

Jn den tagen Asueri des küngs der do regnieret vonn jndia biß zu dem moren lad vber hondert/vñ.xxviij. gögen land oder graff schatz/do er saß jn dē saal od künglichen stůl seines reichs ¶Was susa die stat der anefang seines richs oder seiner regnierong/Darumb er dan jn dē drytten jar seines keiserlichen reichs het ge macht ein grosse wirtschafft allen seinen für sten/edlen/vnd dener/die dan warend die al ler störksten persarum/vnd medoru/seine ed len phleger/vñ amptleut/jn den lender oder lantschafften vor jn/auff dz er yn anzeigen wer die reichtom glori/eer/vnd macht seines reichs. ¶Vil zeit /das ist /hondert.lxxxviij. tag lang. ¶Vnd do die tag der wirtschafft erfült waren/lůd er alles volck das da jn der stat Susis ward erfunden/von dem meisten biß zu dem mynsten/vnnd gebot dz die selbe wirtschafft bereit wirde siben tag lang jn dē

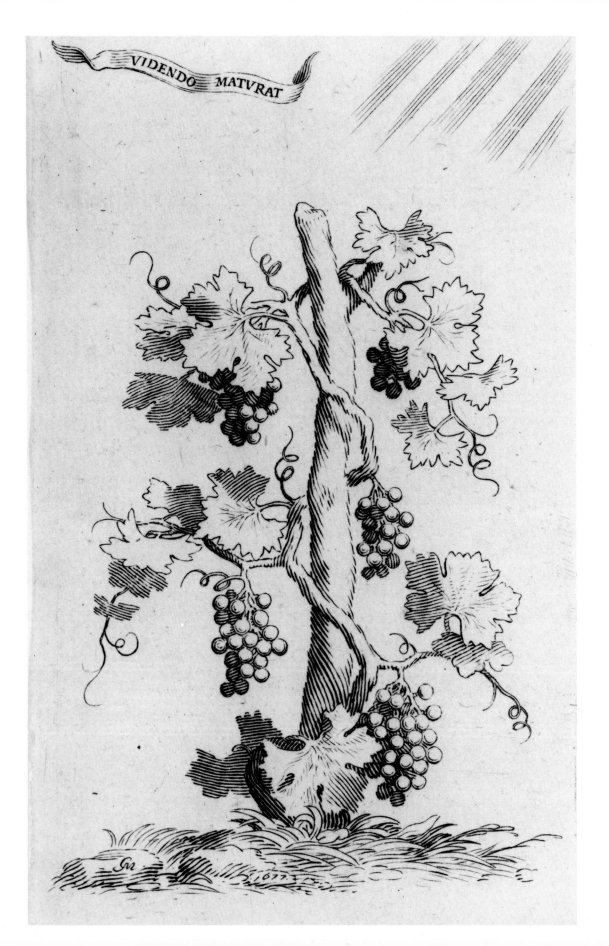

84

VIDENDO MATVRAT

3 The Prolific Grape

Californians who enjoy wine are singularly blessed. In their retail stores, they have access to more than 900 indigenous table wines of the type that are classified as *varietal*. Among them are 32 white wines, such as Pinot Chardonnay, Johannisberg Riesling, Gewürztraminer, Fumé Blanc and Chenin Blanc, and 24 reds, such as Cabernet Sauvignon, Zinfandel, Gamay Noir, and Pinot Noir. As produced by 174 different local wineries, they appear in the marketplace behind 923 individual labels, give or take a few.

This array, impressive as it is, does not include a drop of other American or foreign wines, which are also abundantly available in California. Nor does it take account of any of California's innumerable *generic* wines, such as Burgundy and Chablis, champagnes, sherries, and ports; it refers to only the state's varietal table wines. Despite the long list of premium-quality wines, the grapes for which they are named are sparse producers, and many of the varietal wines are produced in such small quantities that there's not enough to fill the long pipelines to more distant markets.

This is as good a spot as any to review the wine classifications, *varietal* and *generic*, and to examine yet a third.

Varietal wine is produced predominantly from the juice of a single grape variety. If a wine bears the name of a grape, it is a varietal.

Generic is the classification given to a wine with a name that once identified the wine's geographic origin (Burgundy is the classic example), but is now in general use for wines of that type.

Proprietary, the third and growing classification, refers to a distinctive wine produced exclusively by one vintner. It is often a secret blend with an individuality that differs from all other wines.

Opposite
A grapevine, if it is to bear good fruit, must be carefully nurtured to maturity; as is implied by the motto, Videndo Maturat, *in this 1677 engraving by Claude Mellan.* The Christian Brothers Collection.

The Grapevine, *a woodcut by Aristide Maillol is an illustration from a 1950 edition of Vergil's* Georgics. Mr. and Mrs. Alfred Fromm Collection.

Traditionally, some geographically rooted names are used to designate generic wines because the name describes a wine's general characteristics, not because the wine originated in that area. A California Chablis, for example, is a fairly dry white dinner wine, while a California Burgundy is a red table wine.

This method of labeling began with European immigrant vintners of the last century, who gave their wines the names that seemed to fit best. Today, to avoid any misunderstanding, these wines must show their place of origin on the label — such as California, or New York State — in large, clearly legible type directly associated with the generic name.

Two things need to be said here. One is that some of the loveliest premium generic wines are blends of grapes that would achieve distinction behind a varietal label. The other is that neither high price nor pretentious label is a requisite to a pleasant wine experience. Even popularly priced "standard" wines — the American counterpart of Europe's *vins ordinaires* or *vins du pays* (country wines) — enjoy fine reputations among discriminating wine drinkers. In numerous comparisons by experienced wine tasters, they have been found superior to the everyday wines of France and Italy.

Good examples of proprietary wines in the premium-quality category are The Christian Brothers' Château La Salle and Paul Masson's Emerald Dry. Mass-production vintners can point to their big-volume, specially flavored "pop" wines as proprietaries.

Through the ages, artists presented the noble grape in various forms of expression. This sixteenth-century German carved oak-wood relief panel was probably from a choir stall and thus symbolizes the Blood of Christ. Mr. and Mrs. Alfred Fromm Collection.

Nature's Role

Californians are indebted to Mother Nature for this proliferation of wine types. It is she who supplies the sun, the soil, and the climate to grow suitable grapes under conditions most likely to produce elegant wines. In the propagation of the grapes, though, as well as in the process that transforms their juice into wine, Nature has had a good deal of human assistance.

LV.

Vindemia.   Die Weinlese.

Vinum n. 2.	Der Wein	
crescit	wächset	
in *vinea*, 1	in dem Weinberg/ 1	Vinea, f. 1. der Wein= berg.
ubi *vites*	allwo die Weinstöcke	Vitis, f. 3. der Weinstock.
propagantur,	fortgepflanzet/	
& *viminibus*	und mit Weidenruten	Vimen, n. 3. die Wei= denrute.
ad *arbores*, 2	an die Bäume/ 2	Arbor, f. 3. der Baum.
vel ad *palos*, (*ridicas*) (8	oder an die Weinpfä= (le, 3	Palus, m. 2. (Ridica. f. 1.) der Weinpfah' .
vel ad *juga* 4	an die Weinlatten 4	Jugum, n. 2. die Wein= latte.
alligantur	angebunden werden	
Cum *tempus* n. 3. adest	Wenn die Zeit da ist	
vindemiandi,	den Wein zu lesen,	
abscindit *vinitor* m. 3.	schneidet der Winzer	Botrus. m. 2. die
botros,	die Trauben ab.	Traube.

com

Not least among her helpers have been the agricultural scientists at the Davis campus of the University of California near Sacramento — viticulturists, who deal with matters of vine and vineyard and enologists, who are concerned with perfecting winemaking procedures. So highly are these specialists esteemed that quite a few European vintners, with centuries of the finest traditions behind them, choose to send their sons to study with the masters at Davis.

The role of the scientists becomes clear when you realize that in the United States alone more than six thousand varieties of grapes have been identified. Selecting the grapes best suited to wine and most adaptable to genetic modification, performing the botanical marriage called hybridization, and making geological analyses of the soil are some of the functions that University of California experts have performed with distinction.

The six thousand American grape varieties are members of four families, or species. In all the world there are fewer than sixty species of grape, and the scientists tell us that perhaps 75 percent of them are hybrids, crossbred to improve the properties that make them suitable for wine, table use, or raisins. The four species that claim American offspring are: *Vitis labrusca*, as indigenous to American soil as the American Indian; *Vitis vinifera*, a European émigré; *Vitis rotundifolia*; and *Vitis muscadinia*.

Happily, it's possible when dealing with European and most American wines to disregard grape species other than the *vinifera*. Even then,

we are beset with a degree of complexity, for hundreds of different vines belong to this one family. In California alone, official records show sixty-two varieties of *vinifera* grapes planted and harvested — no mean number when we consider that each differs from the rest.

Just as a beginning, *vinifera* varieties differ from one another in their vine growth, leaf shape, color of foliage, and the climatic conditions under which they flourish best. They differ, too, in maturation period, in the number of clusters per vine, the number of berries per cluster, and thus in the tonnage of grapes they yield to the acre. There are variations in even the berry itself — in shape, in size, in the thickness of the skin, in the number of seeds, in the relationship of juice to pulp, and most importantly, in the taste of their juice.

For centuries, European vintners have experimented with the different varieties in an effort to single out the best wine grapes for their operations. They are thus concerned with but a few of the plentiful grape varieties. On the other hand, in comparatively new wine areas such as the United States, while we have already determined which of Europe's accepted grape varieties bring about the best results for us and in what areas they thrive, we are still actively testing other varieties and even, through crossbreeding, creating yet better grapes.

Perhaps we should here back-pedal a bit to that generality about the dominance of the *vinifera* grape in wines. In the eastern United States, less liberally endowed with wine grapes due to the harsher climate, the indigenous wines have always been derived from the juice of the *V. labrusca*. There, too, like our Californian specialists, scientists and vintners have collaborated in the mating of different varieties, including those of *V. vinifera*, to produce new types of wine grapes. The *labrusca* vine, however, as we shall see a bit later, has performed a service of heroic dimensions far beyond supplying juice for eastern wines. It has played a life-saving role that European vineyardists have never forgotten as they tend their *vinifera* vines and harvest their precious *vinifera* grapes.

Opposite
Entitled Die Weinlese (The Vintage), *this woodcut from an eighteenth-century German dictionary carries the explanation that wine grows in the vineyard where the vines are tied to trees or stakes with willow branches. Today, neither trees nor willow branches are used for this purpose.* The Christian Brothers Collection.

Utility Grapes

Least honored among all the grapes that make California wines is one that in some years has accounted for about half the crush — the "utility" grape known as Thompson Seedless. This is an injustice, for the Thompson is a kind of balance wheel in the sometimes chaotic grape-growing business; it is equally at home on your dinner table as fresh fruit, in the package for munching as raisins, or in the fermentation tank for the making of dessert wine and even low-priced table wine.

In the same multipurpose category but far less prolific are the Sultana, the Muscat, and the Black Corinth (or Zante currant). Table grapes — the Emperor, Tokay, White Malaga, among them — contribute their juice for wine in about one-fifth the volume of the Thompson. But those bland grapes lack sufficient flavor and aroma to make premium-quality wine.

Well apart from those we have mentioned stand the special wine varieties bearing the mouth-watering names of Sauvignon Blanc, Grenache, Zinfandel, Gamay, Riesling, Chenin Blanc, Chardonnay, Pinot St. George, Pinot Noir, and Cabernet Sauvignon, to mention only a few of the sixty-two most popular kinds. In their availability for wine-making, these range widely from the twenty thousand tons credited to such shyly bearing grapes as the Pinot Chardonnay and Johannisberg Riesling (white varietals) to the almost two-hundred thousand tons of the red wine grape, Carignane.

New Plantings

Gradually the ratios are changing. The considerable new grapevine plantings in California and other wine-producing states are now almost entirely in varieties used for table wines. In

Opposite
A bunch of grapes is carefully held by the Weinnarr, *or wine jester, in this 1523 engraving by* Lucas van Leyden. *The Christian Brothers Collection.*

Der Rebmann.

Ich bin ein Hácker im Weinberg
Im Früling hab ich harte werck/
Mit graben/ pältzen vnd mit hauwen/
Mit Pfälstossn/ pflantzen vnd bauwen/
Mit auffbinden vnd schneiden die Reben/
Biß im Herbst die Traubn Wein geben:
Den man schneidt vnd außprest deñ fein
Noa erfand erstlich den Wein.

Der Rebmann
The Vineyard Worker
I am a worker in the Vineyard
In Spring I have hard work to do.
With digging, pruning, and with hoeing.
With grafting, planting, and bending.
With binding and cutting the vines.
Until in Fall the grapes give wine.
When they are cut and pressed finely.
Noah first invented the wine.

Just as Jost Amman illustrated in this 1568 woodcut, so even today, much of the year-round labor in the vineyards is still being performed by human hands. The Christian Brothers Collection.

California, these new plantings tripled the acreage of *wine* grapes in ten years. Moreover, wine grapes presently exceed 50 percent of the total California grape acreage and continue to increase their ratio.

What are the conditions, both natural and man-made, that enable the vineyardist to tap this cornucopia, year in and year out? The soil, climate, and water supply are Nature's ingredients, and to some extent the contour of the land, whether it is hilly or flat, is also a factor. Man supplies the knowledge, the muscle, the worry, and the tender, loving care. He is equipped to measure how much of these human contributions he makes, and more and more he is learning how to measure Nature's.

Measuring Climate

The amount of sunshine and warmth the grape gets during the growing season is one of the important criteria for successful vine culture. To measure it precisely, California viticulturists established a system of degree-days by which the state's winegrowing areas are separated into five classes, each best suited to certain grape varieties. Between April and October, the growing season, daily temperature figures are added up — the number of degrees by which the day's average exceeds fifty degrees Fahrenheit. According to this formula, a day on which the average temperature is seventy-five degrees Fahrenheit will add twenty-five degrees to the season's total.

Cumulative totals for a season in the many California vineyard areas run from twenty-five hundred degree-days up, and they tell the experienced grower which grapes will thrive best in which areas. California's coastal area, and especially that section along the northern coast, has a comparatively low degree-day rating, which means that grapes planted there will take longer to mature. Slower maturity, however, yields finer taste and aroma in the fruit, and these in turn enhance the wine. When the degree-day rating is high, as in the great Central Valley from Sacramento to Fresno and Bakers-

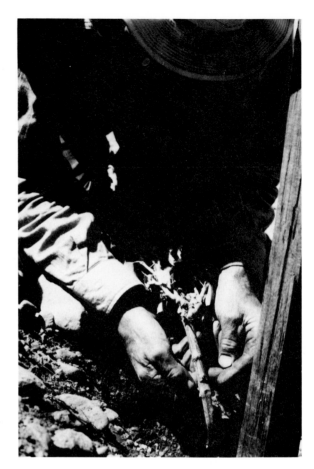

A tender rooting is carefully planted next to a stake. It will be three to four years before the new vine will bear its first fruit. Photo Courtesy Wente Brothers.

Opposite
The various labors of the vineyard throughout the year are the subjects of this series of pen lithographs, mid-nineteenth-century popular cut-out imagery from Vienna. The Christian Brothers Collection.

Druck v F Sieger　　　　　　　　　　　　　　　　　　　　　　　Verlag : M Trentsensky Wien　4

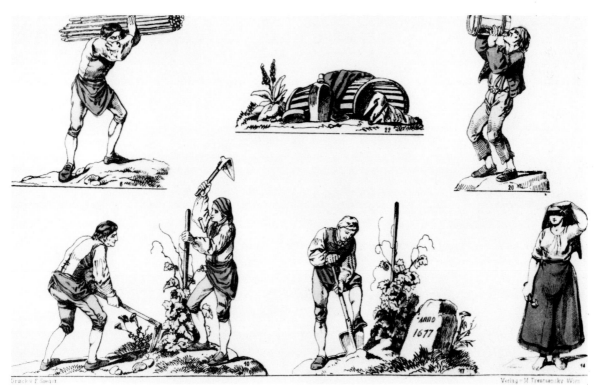

Druck v F Sieger　　　　　　　　　　　　　　　　　　　　　　　Verlag : M Trentsensky Wien

field, the grape matures at a much earlier date — sometimes in August — and must be harvested then. The valley accounts for the entire California crop of Thompson Seedless grapes diverted to wine.

With the abundance of heat usually comes a greater volume of juice, which in turn tends to dilute the flavor and the aroma. Higher heat also means faster evaporation of ground moisture, which calls for more irrigation. Here, ten tons of grapes and more per acre are not uncommon, as compared to two and one-half to five tons per acre on the north coast.

In the past, all operations in the vineyard had to be done by hand — the hoeing, pruning, and weeding as well as the inserting of stakes and the binding of the new branches to the stakes. Today some of this work is done by machines. This pair of broadsides with hand-colored line engravings and text in Latin and German are illustrations from the 1747 Ampelographia Iconica *by Johann Christoph Homann.* The Christian Brothers Collection.

Deep Roots

When you drive alongside a vineyard in winter and see the gnarled black vines, naked of foliage and standing scarcely four or five feet above ground, it's difficult to believe that their roots may reach six to ten feet down — as much as twenty feet if they're desperate for water! The vines can only thrive when the soil is loose enough, with a gravelly quality, to permit that kind of root penetration. And, the roots will continue to push deeper as long as they have to do so to find the water the vine needs.

There is in the Bordeaux region of France an area called Graves. It has a gravelly soil (hence the name), and the story that's told is that the little stones in the soil absorb the heat of the sun during the day, then pass it on to the plant after sunset for additional growing. Many of the finer German wines are grown on mountainsides that are quite gravelly, too.

The geological composition of the soil is also critical. Along the Moselle River in Germany, many vines grow on hills that have a lot of shale in the soil, which you can almost taste in the grape and in the wine. It's a light, almost metallic taste; some might call it flinty. In the region

In La Taille de la Vigne, *a woodcut illustration by Aristide Maillol from a 1950 copy of Vergil's* Georgics, *vineyard workers are shown pruning the vines in winter.* The Christian Brothers Collection.

of France known as Champagne, the soil is fairly chalky and the Champagne growers claim that it's the chalky soil that gives their sparkling wine its unique flavor.

Urban and even rural Americans, reared in the tradition that friable coal-black loam is the *sine qua non* of successful agriculture, rarely fail to be shocked when they see the soil in some of California's most prestigious vineyards. Often it has the color of yellow clay, which it is not, and is so rocky that it would seem to defy plant life. On the contrary, given enough water, the odd soil only encourages the vines to do their best. It also produces an abundant crop of weeds. To the uninitiated visitor, there is hardly a lovelier sight than a vineyard in spring wearing a golden mantle of mustard — an unwelcome intruder that taxes the grower's capacity for the care and nurture of his crop. The luxuriant coverlet of gold is Nature's response to the winter's rains.

After the winter pruning, the vine shoots are gathered to propagate new vines, usually in a nursery. This chore is depicted in Jeunes Filles Remassant des Sarments de Vigne, *another woodcut illustration by Aristide Maillol from a 1950 edition of* Vergil's Georgics. The Christian Brothers Collection.

During the second half of the nineteenth century, Chinese laborers, returning from building the transcontinental railroad, worked in California's vineyards and wineries. This wood-engraved illustration from the November, 1884, issue of Frank Leslie's Popular Monthly shows Chinese picking grapes in a mountain vineyard. The cart transported the grapes to the winery. The Christian Brothers Collection.

Water Supply

The growing popularity of wines has, of course, precipitated a surge of commercial interest in the development of new vineyard properties. A seasoned investor knows that if there's no evidence of adequate water supply, a property has very limited potential as a vineyard. It's too late to make the discovery of a shortage of water after the vines are in.

In this woodcut illustration entitled Les Vendanges *by Aristide Maillol from a 1950 edition of Vergil's* Georgics, *the man is shown taking charge of the heavy collection drum for transport to the winery while two women bring in their full harvest baskets.* The Christian Brothers Collection.

Young women of Tivoli are shown harvesting grapes in this graphite and watercolor drawing by an anonymous Italian artist, dated about 1820. Then, as now, women participated in the grape picking while the men carried grape-laden baskets to the carts and crushers. The Christian Brothers Collection.

Gez. u. lith v. Bülow.   Eigenth. u. Verlag v. Carl Nöhring in Berlin.   Druck v. W. Loeillot in Berlin.

DIE WEINLEESE.

October.

This painted porcelain figurine made in Vienna, Austria, around the middle of the eighteenth century depicts a young vintager in a nobleman's costume. He holds a vintager's knife in his right hand while standing next to a grape-laden basket. 7¼" high. The Christian Brothers Collection.

How much water is desirable? An accepted rule of thumb is that it takes from sixteen to thirty inches of rainfall per year or the equivalent in irrigation water to grow good wine grapes successfully. If annual rainfall in a given area is only ten inches, then the grower must supply the additional six to twenty inches if he hopes for optimum yield. In some of Europe's most celebrated growing areas, the vineyardist hopes that enough rain will fall, at the right time, to encourage the vines to produce the best fruit. When, during the growing season, there's not enough sun and too little or too much rain, a poor vintage is harvested — poor in quality, in quantity, or in both.

In California, the situation is quite different. Along the state's north coast, there is generally enough — or almost enough — rain for the vines' needs. On the occasions when the annual precipitation does not reach a suitable level, man has provided light overhead sprinklers that supply additional moisture. In other parts of California, especially in the state's hot Central Valley, irrigation of vines, as of all agriculture, is a constant necessity.

Irrigation of the valley vineyards does not generally consist of flowing water through a network of ditches, which is the way orchards and field crops are normally irrigated. Rather, until recent years, it involved the use of sprinklers hooked up to enormous lengths of pipe that workers placed by hand and then moved to the next location when a given area was covered. On a large spread in the valley, applying needed water by means of such a "portable" system became an exercise in human engineering.

Overhead Spray

Inevitably the portable sprinkler system is giving way to what's known as "permanent-set" irrigation, an underground network of pipes feeding overhead sprinklers spaced to supply optimum spray coverage. The flick of a switch or the turn of a single valve can bathe an entire vineyard in mist. With agricultural labor increasingly at a premium, the operational simplicity of permanent-set irrigation has obvious advan-

— Imbècile de vendangeur !....faites donc attention à ce que vous faites !...
— Pardon , madame , j'ai cru que c'était la tonne !......

tages in supplying vines with the water they need.

Irrigation, however, is only one of the several benefits attributed to the overhead sprinkler system. It is in fact a year-round vineyard aid. In early spring, when new growth starts to appear on the vines, low temperatures are a grave hazard, and at the freezing level the tender buds of the forthcoming crop are in jeopardy. In the past, some vineyardists used (and continue to use) smudge pots with moderate success to lift the ambient temperature during a cold wave. Others have used (and likewise continue to use) high-powered fans in the vineyard to blow warmer currents of air over the vines and so

Actualités 443: — Imbècile de vendangeur! . . . faites donc attention à ce que vous faites! . . . — Pardon, madame, j'ai cru que c'était la tonne! . . . (Actualities 443: _— Stupid vintager! . . . why don't you watch what you are doing? — Pardon me, madam, I thought that this was the vat. . . ._)

Cham (Amédée Charles Henri, comte de Noé) ridicules the ladies' fashionable hoopskirts in this nineteenth-century lithograph from Charivari. The Christian Brothers Collection.

Brentator da Vino.

Opposite
This etching by Simon Guillain (after a drawing by
Annibale Carracci) was published in Rome in 1646.
Captioned Brentator da Vino (Wine Porter), *it*
actually pictures a grape porter carrying the grapes
from the mountain vineyards. The curvature of the
basket serves to distribute the heavy weight on the
man's back and to facilitate the dumping of
the grapes into the crusher. The Christian Brothers
Collection.

A late-nineteenth-century team of grape pickers at
Mission San José in Alameda County, California. The
pickers emptied their baskets into the large drums
by the side of the road where horse-drawn wagons
loaded them for delivery to the winery. Photo
courtesy Weibel Vineyards.

This painted tôle vintager, shown eating a grape from a bunch taken from the basket on her back, was chosen by a mid-nineteenth-century Austrian artist as the mask for an otherwise uninteresting umbrella stand. 27″ high. The Christian Brothers Collection.

he turns on his sprinklers, the vines are showered with a spray that becomes a cloak of ice on the tender new shoots, thus protecting them from temperatures that would otherwise kill them. This preventive action is effective down to temperatures as low as twenty-four degrees Fahrenheit, if the cold snap doesn't last more than a few days. A vineyard wearing an overcoat of ice in the spring is an unforgettable picture; more practically, the crystal mantle can literally be a crop saver.

In the north coastal area of California, known for the quality table wines it produces, there are vintners who have equipped their long-established premium-grape vineyards with permanent-set irrigation. Their investment is returned in full by their savings in one severe frost, especially since frost-damaged vines sometimes carry into the second crop year an incapacity to bear a full crop. For protecting less expensive grapes, of course, the saving would be less spectacular, but usually still very worthwhile.

The fixed-position overhead sprinklers offer yet another advantage — in the summer they shield the crop against the threat posed by immoderate heat. Especially in the coastal valleys where summer evenings are cool and grapes can literally loaf to maturity, sudden waves of excessive heat can cause heat injury to the berries, even subject whole clusters to sunburn and heat shrivel. A timely man-made shower can take the sting out of the heat wave and prevent severe crop damage by lowering vineyard temperatures as much as eight to ten degrees.

No matter how primitive his husbandry, the successful vineyardist has always had to function as an engineer as well. He can, after all, plant his vines only after he has determined that all of the conditions bearing on the success of his enterprise are hospitable. With the rising de-

ward off the killing frost. Such measures are but temporary expedients, however, and even with their application, a deep and continuing cold wave can bring crop damage and heavy losses.

A vineyardist with an overhead sprinkler system and an adequate water supply has the best method so far devised for fighting frost. When

Opposite
The contemporary Swiss artist, Hans Erni, presents two grape pickers in this etching. The Christian Brothers Collection.

In this early seventeenth-century Dutch engraving
from a series of the four seasons, Jacob Matham
presents Autumnus bringing the grapes and fruits of
the harvest beneath the signs of the zodiac. The
Christian Brothers Collection.

mand for wine grapes, possession of this trait has become ever more vital; it reaches a peak of importance when he lays out a new vineyard today.

Comparing Costs

The mercurial Hungarian, "Count" Agoston Haraszthy de Mokesa, who in 1856 bought the Buena Vista ranch in Sonoma, left us a record of the high cost of growing, circa 1858, the year he planted a one-hundred-acre spread in the shadow of General Mariano Vallejo's Lachryma Montis vineyard. Year by year, for three years until the vines started to bear, he jotted down his costs, starting the first year with: Six men @ $1.93 per day wages and board to handle the teams for 20 days of deep plowing; 15 horses, 75 cents a day each, 20 days; 18 men

Grape picking and winemaking are among the activities of autumn depicted in this sixteenth-century engraving by Philip Galle (after Maarten van Heemskerck). The Christian Brothers Collection.

@ \$1.73 per day wages and board, for 21 days of laying out the vineyard, staking and digging holes; 68,000 rooted vines, ¼-cent each. In the second year, the Buena Vista vintner recorded an expense familiar to all vineyardists: replacing the young vines that died, \$60. And, in both the second and third years, Haraszthy reported pruning and summer cultivation as the big costs.

The three-year total for Haraszthy's hundred acres of vines, now ready to yield a small first crop, was \$4,019.64 — the "count" meticulously included the pennies — or \$40.20 per acre. If we assume that Haraszthy paid \$35 an acre for the raw land, we may conclude that his grape costs for the first vintage of Buena Vista wine under his proprietorship were very modest, at least by today's standards. The cost for a north-coast-area vineyard of identical size planted today would be one hundred to two hundred times as great.

Consider the density of Haraszthy's planting: 680 vines per acre, allowing each vine 64 square feet of "territory" in an 8 × 8 grid — 8 feet between vines and 8 feet between rows. That

During the late spring, vines growing on the east side of the Santa Clara Valley are shown growing on individual stakes; some younger vines were planted to replace destroyed ones. Photo courtesy Mirassou Vineyards.

could well have been the standard spacing of that era, and Haraszthy could have brought the practice from Europe or the eastern United States. It was thought at the time that the more vines you crowded into an acre of land, the greater your grape harvest and, of course, the greater your volume of wine production. Modern growers in California's coastal valleys discovered the fallacy of that by removing, as an experiment, every second vine in a densely (7 × 7 feet) planted vineyard. Within three years, the grape yield from half as many vines rose to the same level as before.

Some mountain vineyards are so steep and densely planted that they have to be worked with horses or by manpower.

XXXIV

Vigne d'amerique   *P. Sluyter sculp.*

One of the vines of early colonial America is visually
captured by the eighteenth-century Dutch artist,
Pieter Sluyter, in this hand-colored line engraving
titled simply Vigne d'Amérique (American Vine),
published in 1705. Later, the number of different
vines found in the New World necessitated that they
be given more specific names. The Christian
Brothers Collection.

Opposite
*Wasps are attracted by the sweet juice of ripening
grapes in* La Guepe, *an aquatint etching by Pablo
Picasso from the illustrations of Buffon's* Natural
History, *executed in the late 1930s.* Mr. and Mrs.
Alfred Fromm Collection.

Vintage in the Abruzzi, *a late-nineteenth-century hand-colored lithograph by Englishman, Thomas Allom, depicts a colorful harvest scene in this mountainous coastal area of Italy. The man in the background picks the grape clusters from tree-clinging vines, which the woman carries in a heavy-laden basket on her head.* The Christian Brothers Collection.

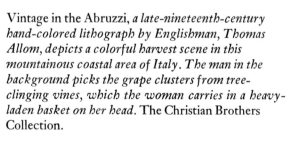

Two young vintagers carefully fill a large bucket with grapes in this nineteenth-century Italian porcelain figure group from the Capo di Monte factory near Naples. 7½″ high. The Christian Brothers Collection.

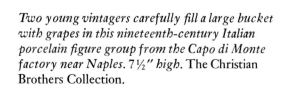

Spaced for Machines

Today, a common density for varieties of vigorous growth in the high-quality Napa-Sonoma-Mendocino area of California is 454 vines per acre with vines 8 feet apart and 12 feet between rows. Not only is that spacing calculated to give the roots and the vines elbowroom and more exposure to the sun, but it adapts readily to the covering power of permanent-set irrigation and to the use of the tractors that have replaced horses in cultivating.

Putting aside the custom of the mid-nineteenth century to crowd one-half more vines into a given space than is the accepted custom today, it's worth noting that Haraszthy — like his twentieth-century counterpart — found no shortcut for acquiring and planting his vines. "Thirty-two days' work was spent in digging the rooted vines in the nursery," he reported, with a touch of asperity. "Their cultivation in the summer brought their cost to one-quarter of a cent each." In addition to the 18 men laying out the grid pattern, driving stakes to support the vines as they grew, and digging holes to receive the 68,000 rooted cuttings, he had another 6 following behind and planting the cuttings, then firming the soil around the tender roots.

Except for a little mechanization — such as the hydraulic drilling of holes to receive the cuttings — the planting routine hasn't changed much in over a century. Vineyardists still rely on cuttings from proved vines to plant in the holes drilled alongside the geometrically positioned stakes; almost nobody outside a viticultural laboratory propagates vines from seeds. Growers may buy disease-resistant cuttings commercially from nurseries, or they may propagate their own from the small branches they prune from the vines in the winter. These branches, which formerly were burned and their ashes spread as fertilizer, are slender whips of wood. The cuttings, or shoots, are planted in a sheltered environment, where in a year they sprout tiny roots. They're then ready to be transplanted in a vineyard, the fragile roots about a foot below the surface and the whip projecting about six inches above. Growth is gradual — a foot or a foot and a half the first year; as much again the second year. Each winter the young plants must be expertly pruned and tied to the stake. It takes at least three years, and in the cooler climates of the premium districts, four years, for the first fruit to appear.

Foiling the Wildlife

As fresh cuttings, the vines are vulnerable to the mischief of the rabbits and deer that feast on their tender foliage. To thwart the wildlife, the grower encloses each plant with a little box, such as a milk carton, open at both ends. The white paper cartons beside the tall stakes are a study in composition in a new vineyard.

It's true, of course, that older vineyards are not staked. And, when you examine the rugged trunks of some of those old vines, you can see no reason why they should be; some are as firm as a locust tree and have the low profile of a bandy-legged prize fighter. Stakes do lend support to young vines, but their function goes well beyond that. Standing alone, and with crossarms like utility poles, they provide support to branches of the mature vines when their precious burden of fruit would otherwise make them sag to the ground and thus expose them to more pests. The modern practice has been to stretch wires along the crossarms to create a continuous trellis that will support the fruit-bearing branches.

Denuded Stumps

It's a little sad to see a vine or a vineyard after it has yielded up its fruit. Soon after the grapes are harvested, the vine seems to relax,

Bacchus réduit à boire du Coco par suite de la Maladie des Raisins.

fold up. The green foliage edges into autumnal shades, and then the leaves fall. Within two or three weeks, the vineyard seems to be going to sleep. And, in a sense, it is, for the vine is dormant in winter, and the vineyard, stripped of its gay summer garments, takes on the gaunt appearance of a forest after a fierce artillery engagement.

If the denuded vines are a sign that one vintage is over, they are equally a signal that a new vintage is in the making. While the vines are resting, the vineyardist is not; grape growing is a year-round occupation. In winter, as weather permits, the vineyardist deploys his ex-perienced workers among the vines to prune the long tendrils of the past year's growth, leaving only a selected few per vine to become the heart of next summer's crop. The whips of growth the vineyard workers remove are not discarded. They are carefully collected and tagged for identification, for they will become, after they're rooted in the nursery, tomorrow's new vine plantings. The identification tags are important for several reasons. One is that growers favor cuttings from mother vines that yield the best or the most grapes. Another is that if the mother vine becomes diseased and must be destroyed, her progeny can be traced by the

Actualités 75: Bacchus reduit à boire du coco par suit de la maladie des raisins. (Actualities 75: *Bacchus reduced to drinking cocoa as a result of the grape disease*). Phylloxera, *the dreaded blight that struck European vineyards and destroyed more than half of the French vineyards in the 1870s, is parodied in this cartoon from the satirical review* Charivari *by Cham (Amédée Charles Henri comte de Noé), a contemporary of Honoré Daumier.* The Christian Brothers Collection.

Actualités 397. Les Inquiétudes du Viticulteur: — Nous venons d'échapper à la gelée . . . nous n'avons plus à craindre que le soleil, la plui, l'oidium, et le reste! . . . (Actualities 397. The Anxieties of the Winegrower: — *Now that we have avoided the frost . . . all we have to worry about are the sun, the rain, the grape disease, and all the rest! . . .*)

Honoré Daumier produced numerous cartoons parodying the changing fortunes of the winegrower and the vintner. In this lithograph from an 1857 issue of Charivari, *the winegrower in spring, having survived the freeze, contemplates the future.* The Christian Brothers Collection.

LES INQUIÉTUDES DU VITICULTEUR .
_ Nous venons d'échapper à la gelée.... nous n'avons plus à craindre que le soleil, la pluie, l'oïdium, et le reste!...

Beneath the Vine or Figtrees.

tags and also uprooted to prevent the spread of the disease to other vines.

Guiding Growth

Pruning requires judgment and skill. The vineyard worker is trained to retain the branches that determine the direction of the vine's desired growth, and to remove those branches that would steer it along the wrong path. Stray branches dissipate the juice that rises from the root. The surviving canes are then tied either to the stake or to the trellis wire to guide their future growth.

"April showers bring May flowers." So runs the children's couplet. Grape growers could paraphrase that to "Winter rains bring weeding pains." To preserve the soil's moisture and nutrition for the vines, the weeds must be hoed and turned under every spring. And while that operation is under way, the grower must keep an eye on the weather, for after the first few warm days, little buds appear on the vines, to be followed soon by tender new leaves, and this new growth is terribly vulnerable to frost. Should the thermometer head down toward freezing level, he had better be prepared to unlimber his frost-protection measures, whether they be smudge pots, high-velocity fans, or overhead sprinklers that shroud the vines in ice. Unseasonal cold snaps in northern California have cost inadequately protected vineyards as much as 40 percent of their vintage.

It's a viticultural fact of life that the vines that give the finest, most flavorful grapes in California's north coast districts are more sensitive to the cold than those producing more prosaic fruit. The native *labrusca* vines of the eastern and midwestern United States, for example, are obviously much hardier than California's *vinifera* varieties because they easily survive the extreme winters of their areas.

Enemies of the Vine

Weeds and frost are only two of the enemies the grower must battle to protect his fruit. From the time the first leaves appear in the spring, he must maintain an alert against rabbits, deer, and other critters on the prowl for a free meal. And, once the berries displace the blossoms and begin to generate sugar and juice, birds will make a convention center of a vineyard if they're not dispersed. In Europe, growers will sometimes cover their vines with netting or plastic film to thwart the birds. Some American vineyardists, aware that the feathered creatures can steal as much as 10 or 20 percent of the crop, have resorted to rotating poles carrying loudspeakers that broadcast the sounds of menacing animals or predatory birds. Unless they change recorded sounds every week or so, though, the birds lose their fear.

Like any farmer, the grape grower must fight insects and parasites, including nematodes and grape lice. From spring through harvest, the vines and the grapes tempt a multitude of pests that must be controlled by spraying and dusting.

The pest that seemed uncontrollable when it came to the fore in the mid-nineteenth century was the grapevine root-louse we have mentioned before called *Phylloxera*. In the 1870s and 1880s, it almost literally wiped out the vineyards of France and did extreme damage to those of Germany, Spain, Italy, and other European countries. In California, it left its mark but not to the decimating extent that it did throughout Europe.

Phylloxera, it turned out, while it loved the roots of the *vinifera*, scorned those of the native American *labrusca*, and this proved to be the saving grace for much of Europe's wineland. The growers of the Old Country imported *labrusca* cuttings and used them as rootstocks to which they grafted their *vinifera*. In California, too, the use of rootstocks became a pretty general pattern, and while today some growers will establish a vineyard of *vinifera* vines on their own roots ("direct producers," they are called), the general pattern is either to set out recognized *labrusca* rootstocks and graft the *vinifera* to them, or to purchase them so grafted from a nursery.

Sugar-Acid Ratio

Of all the judgmental decisions confronting the grower in the twelve-month cycle from harvest to harvest, none is more critical than when to gather in the crop. If he does so too early, the grapes will be immature; if too late, they may be overripe. In either case, the wine will suffer. So he watches through the summer as the grapes change in color from light to dark green, to yellow, pink, red, purple, black. As the critical time approaches, he tastes them; his aim is to achieve optimum balance between acid and sugar.

For a precise measurement, he carries in his pocket an instrument not much larger than a jack-knife. He inserts one berry in the instrument, presses a button that pushes a needle into the berry. The hand refractometer, used in preliminary field tests, automatically tells him the sugar content, which in the United States is expressed in terms of degrees Balling. Shortly before the beginning of harvesting, more exacting and separate tests are made of the clear juice from sample clusters of each grape variety, taken at various locations in the vineyard. These tests are usually made with a hydrometer in a large, cylindrical glass. The desired sugar content in grapes intended for table wines of 12 percent alcohol strength is about twenty-two degrees Balling. If it's much higher—that is, if the grape is too sweet—it may upset the critical balance between sugar and acid.

Not always can the grower wait for the sun to bring the sugar content to the ideal level and the grapes to full maturity. In European vineyards, especially those in cool northern latitudes of France, Germany, and Switzerland, the maturing period bumps into the start of the colder rainy season. The wary grower, to avoid the hazards of rainfall or frost, will often harvest his crop before the grapes are fully ripened. The American vintner, in contrast, finds that even in what he would call a "poor" year, the grapes reach a fully acceptable maturity.

Clearly, the uncertainties of this specialized kind of agriculture call for a high degree of professionalism. In California alone, there are upwards of ten thousand growers who sell their wine-variety grapes to the state's licensed wineries, numbering more than 340.* One group, the Allied Grape Growers, is one of the largest agricultural cooperatives in California, with its 1,500 members selling their grapes to a single wine company, United Vintners.

Grape Grower's Risk

A few pages back, we had a glimpse of the financial commitment a nineteenth-century grape grower had to make. The ebullient Haraszthy, accounting for every penny, said it cost him a little over forty dollars an acre, exclusive of land cost, to prepare and plant and maintain a hundred acres of vines in Sonoma during the three years he waited for his first harvest.

Most of California's ten thousand growers operate vineyards smaller than the one Haraszthy planted for his Buena Vista winery in January, 1858, and the results of their labors and investments are not always very rewarding. A few years ago, a severe April frost caught many growers unprepared, and some vineyardists lost 25 percent, and a few as much as 40 percent, of their crop. Their return for the year sharply reduced their long-term average income.

There is yet another factor to consider. Recent years have seen vast increases in acreages planted to grapes that are in high demand, such as Cabernet Sauvignon, Pinot Noir, and Pinot Chardonnay, all commanding premium prices. It's not unreasonable to expect that at some

*As of January, 1980, there were 377 premises licensed to produce wine in California (676 total in the U.S.). There were also some thousands of amateur winemakers. These formed a substantial market for vintners who produce grape-juice concentrate.

point, the demand for one grape variety will be satisfied, while there will be a simultaneous shortage in another variety. Considering that it takes four years from the planting of the vines to the first harvest, the grape grower has to estimate the demand for each grape variety many years ahead in order to properly decide which varieties to plant and in what quantities.

The choice of good vineyard land depends on soil, water, climate, and weather. More than thirty states now have vineyards, but in many, the growing of the *vinifera* grape is riskier than it is in California. Here again, some areas are more prom-

ising than others for obtaining the best results in the cultivation of particular grape varieties. Coastal valleys produce more flavorful grapes than the Central Valley; along the north coast, the Napa Valley enjoys universal recognition as the foremost wine producing area.

The demand for good California wine has been growing steadily and the increasing supply of grapes has kept in step with this growth. The supply and demand ratio, however, varies from year to year and affects the prices the grower can get for his grapes.

4 The Harvest

For every grower of the grape, there comes at the end of the long twelve-month cycle his moment of truth. It is the moment when, for better or worse, he signals the foreman of his vineyard to let the harvest commence. Now he will learn, when the grapes are gathered and delivered to the crusher, how great or how small is to be the reward for his year's labors. After he pays all the bills, will there be enough left from the sale to salt away a little against the unforeseeable lean year?

Even though he has only a hundred acres of vines, if they are in premium-quality varietal grapes, his crop should be in the neighborhood of four hundred tons of grapes, plus or minus, depending on the varieties. The question is, How much plus or how much minus?

He is not completely in the dark. He undoubtedly kept a running check on the potential size of his crop as the warm sun coaxed the grapes toward maturity. And, when the grape sugar approached, say, twenty degrees Balling, he almost certainly ran precise sugar tests in his laboratory, measuring sugar level, acid content, and other vital statistics of the maturing fruit.

What he was probing for, of course, were the telltale signs that the sugar-acid ratio for the particular variety was at the point where the grapes would produce a superior wine. When his laboratory instruments told him such was the case — and when, as is the grower's habit, he confirmed this with his own taste buds — that was the moment he told his foreman, "Tomorrow we start picking."

Opposite
In this lithograph dated 1894 by Walter Crane, the musical rhythms of the dancer with cymbals is captured through the flowing lines of the draughtsman. The Christian Brothers Collection.

Si, quæ sim, quæris; frons succi plena decori
 Et fronti suggar corporis uber ait.
Quacunque ingredior tellus pinguedine nostra
 Turgida dat manibus dat capitiq. decus.

Illius officio gremium bona copia replet;
 Omnigena pascens os oculosq dape.
Farrea Spectator genitrix et origo tuarq.
 Lætitiæ tuc vita fida columna. CERES.

Carloche Pinx   M de Jager Sculp   A Blooteling Excudit Cum Privilegis Ordinum Hollandiæ et West-Frisiæ

In this lovely late-seventeenth-century engraving by Michel de Jager (after a painting by Carlouche), Ceres displays her harvest, prominent among which are the luscious grapes. The Christian Brothers Collection.

Once that decision was made, it did not mean that the vineyardist's worries were over. There is always, at harvest time, the imponderable of weather conditions, particularly the threat of rain. Normally, this is not too much of an autumn hazard in California's vineyards, but in the northerly latitudes of France, Germany, and Switzerland—where the cool fall days and chilly nights often stretch the grape-maturing process into November—the danger is great that damaging winter rains will arrive before the crop has been picked. If weather forecasts and the grower's judgment tell him rain is on the way, he will gather in his harvest even though he knows the grapes could comfortably use a few more days on the vine.

Rarely is the decision a simple one to make. It will be conditioned to some extent by the availability of a harvesting crew; quite likely the grower's neighbors are confronted by an identical dilemma, and if they all want to harvest at the same time, there may not be enough pickers to go around.

Fortunately, in distributing her bounty, Nature did not decree that all varieties of grapes mature at the same time. Hence, a vineyardist growing four different varieties of wine grapes may be able to harvest them successively over a period of several weeks. There are among California winegrowers some vineyardists with thousands of acres of bearing vines producing eighteen or more varieties of grapes. For them,

This late sixteenth-century Dutch engraving by Philip Galle (after Johannes Stradanus) vividly portrays the many winery activities of the harvest season in autumn. The Christian Brothers Collection.

OCTOBER.   MENSIS X.
MASSICA DISPOSITIS SPVMAT VINDEMIA LABRIS, VITIFERAM PRÆDATVR HVMVM BACCHVMQTRIVMPHAT
PRESSAQ. PVRPVREO RORE FALERNA FLVVNT   EBRIÁQ. IN PRÆLO PRÆLIA MENSIS HABET.
P. Cand. pinx. ab Amling delin et Sulp 1702

In this engraving dated 1702 by Karl Gustav Amling (after a painting by Peter Candid) entitled October, *men and women are shown busily picking, crushing, and sampling the grape harvest.* The Christian Brothers Collection.

the staggered maturities are providential because they are usually able to space out the entire sequence of operations from harvesting through crushing and fermentation.

Community Affair

In some European winegrowing regions, an official beginning of the harvest is announced; in some areas, the picking dates for different grape varieties are specified. This relieves the individual grape grower of the responsibility of making the decision himself, although he will bear the consequences, favorable or not. This official go-ahead signal is especially practiced in areas where there are many small growers whose grapes should be delivered to the crusher at about the same time.

The story is told of a French vintner in California who, because he intended to blend the wines from several varieties of grapes, decided to let Nature do the job for him instead by mixing the vines in the vineyard. His moment of truth came at harvest. Since the different varieties matured at different times, the grape pickers had to direct their steps through the vineyard once for each variety. Even if the tale is apocryphal, it illustrates the diverse characteristics of the grape in its many incarnations.

However sobering the economic realities of the harvest, there is an aura of gaiety associated with the harvest that borders on the carnival. In the United States, it doesn't often reach the level of a district-wide block party, but in parts of Europe, the harvest festival is virtually a regional holiday, with singing, dancing, gay costumes, concerts, processions of lavishly decorated floats — and, of course, wine. In the Swiss cantons of Neuchâtel and Vaud on the French border, they have a name for the harvest celebration that honors their superb wines. They call it *la Fête des Vendanges*. Along the Rhine in Germany, the festival is hailed as *das Winzerfest* by the merrymakers.

The French, too, and the Italians, steeped as they are in the traditions of wine, observe like rituals. They honor not only the farmer who grows the grapes but the vintner who crushes and ferments them, the cooper in whose casks the wines are blended, aged, and finished, and the restaurateur who serves them. Small wonder that the consumer cheerfully crowds into the act.

Like Mardi Gras

In the intensity of the observance and its power to attract every segment of the rural population from the affluent to the peasant, the harvest festival bears a resemblance to the pre-Lenten Mardi gras. Oddly, though, it never degenerates into a drunken orgy, although the wine flows freely. Like the American observance of Thanksgiving, which originated as a reverent bow to the Almighty for Plymouth Colony's bountiful crop, the harvest festival started as an acknowledgment of divine intervention in behalf of the grapes. Over the centuries it has lost some of the religious patina, but in Italy and parts of France, and more recently in some parts of California, a ritualistic blessing of the grapes is still an annual affair.

The romance associated with the annual harvest of wine grapes is not hard to understand, for almost universally the wine that results is the beverage of romance, blushing shyly beneath the veil of mystery that cloaks its creation. And, there's something picturesque about a company of chattering grape pickers as they move down the rows of vines with their shears or their half-moon-shaped knives, snipping the clusters and depositing them in containers that will be dumped into hoppers or gondolas for transport to the winery.

Not All Romance

The romance of harvesting is pretty much in the eyes of the beholder, however, for hand-picking grapes is hard work. In California and around the Mediterranean at least, if not in some of Europe's northerly vineyards with late harvests, the sun is ablaze in an azure sky, the soil is hot to the touch — as it must be to stimulate the rise in the fruit's sugar content — and the grapes dangling from branches all around the vine seem to be playing hide-and-seek with the pickers. He — or she, because picking crews include women and often are family groups with as many as three generations represented — must physically explore under the foliage for the hidden bunches, and the leaves, too, are hot. If the vines haven't been trellised, the burden of fruit will press some of the branches to the ground, and this means stooping over to find and cut the clusters.

Ordinarily, the harvesting teams are paid by the ton of grapes picked. Experienced harvesters are usually part of the pool of farm labor that moves from crop to crop. They're trained to do this hard work, are accustomed to the long hours, which in turn mean larger incomes. In mountain vineyards that are difficult to harvest, they're more likely to be paid an hourly wage than on a volume basis.

In Europe, the teams are almost certain to be

Die Weinlese, Skizze von J. Dielmann.

family groups—and, what's more, working their own vineyards, usually much, much smaller than the vineyards we see in California and upstate New York. Some of the vineyards along the Moselle, and in Burgundy and Bordeaux have only two to two and a half acres of grapes and have been in the same family for generations. In France, many farms were split away from baronial estates as a consequence of the French Revolution, truly a redistribution of the wealth on a massive scale. In these small but productive vineyards, wage rates have no bearing on the work. Everybody in the family participates, not only in the harvest but in the care of the vines and the soil during the dormant and growing seasons, and it's not uncommon to find several generations of a single family sifting through the vines at harvest.

Mostly, these small European viticultural enterprises sell their grapes rather than attempt to crush, ferment, age, bottle, and sell a finished product. They have the option of selling them directly to one of the numerous vintners in their district, or to a growers' cooperative, which makes the wine and divides the proceeds of its sale among co-op members.

Picking by Machine

Some of the mass-production vineyards around the world have in recent years begun to pick their grapes—in part or in whole—by mechanical harvester, a lumbering behemoth of the fields that enables three or four workers to do the work of forty. Like the mechanical harvester of cotton and the machine that now sweeps through a field of ripe tomatoes, the grape harvester did not spring full-blown overnight from a miracle factory. It was the outgrowth of an idea that almost simultaneously struck the agriculturally innovative campuses of Cornell University and the University of California at Davis.

From their work, augmented by that of commercial engineers, came a number of mobile grape harvesters that work on the principle of striking or shaking the vine to make it drop its fruit onto an apron. It is conveyed from the apron to parallel-moving, tractor-drawn gondolas and thence to the winery.

These huge machines—they stand up to twelve feet high—straddle a row of vines and move down the row at a rate that permits them to cover about one acre per hour. Most of the mechanical pickers require nearly level land to work properly, but the recent development of a self-leveling unit (now being used in France) allows the picker to operate on slopes up to

Opposite top
Die Weinlese, *a late-nineteenth-century lithograph by Franz Heister (after a sketch by Jakob Fürchtegott Dielmann) illustrates a grape harvest in the Franconia district of Germany. The man at left firing the rifle is scaring away grape-eating birds. In the upper and lower margins are views of towns on the Main River, including Frankfurt.* The Christian Brothers Collection.

Opposite bottom
Horse-drawn wagons, loaded with lugs full of freshly picked wine grapes, posed for this photograph before delivering the grapes to the crusher. The young man near the one-horse cart is Ernest Wente, working as an apprentice, about 1910. Photo courtesy Wente Brothers.

twenty-five degrees. In addition to harvesting the grapes, the machines are reportedly capable of spraying the vines during the growing season. It is no exaggeration to say that the men of science and the practical engineers have combined talents to bring about what could be called a twentieth-century vineyard revolution.

Despite the advent of the mechanical harvester, the great majority of vineyards in the United States, especially the smaller and older ones, continue to be harvested manually. This is especially true of the picturesque hillside plantings that grace some of the winegrowing areas of this and other countries. Initially, the use of hillsides for the growing of grapes was not a voluntary choice. Far back in history, France and Germany reserved the rich bottom lands of their river valleys to grow grain, field crops, and other foods more urgently needed than grapes, which were thus relegated to the slopes. Vineyardists converted what seemed to be a liability to an asset by claiming — with more than a grain of truth — that hillside locations, especially those with southern exposure, allowed the beneficent warmth of the sun to reach the foliage of the vines at a better angle and bestow that extra kiss on the leaves that helps produce a superior fruit.

Terraced Hillsides

It's worth a small digression here to note that many hillside vineyards in Europe are being converted to miniature "flatlands" by terracing. As some of the older vines die or decline in productivity, vineyardists tear them out and break up the sloping ground into "steps," sometimes with "treads" wide enough for several rows of vines. The terraces are better drained, they're easier to cultivate, and they're not nearly so difficult to harvest.

While, as noted earlier, some mechanical harvesters can be operated on hillsides of limited slopes, there remain many vineyards, both in the United States and elsewhere, where the use of such a harvester or other mechanical equipment is impractical. One positive side of the mechanical harvesting of grapes, as pointed out by those who use it, is that the needed trellis-wires guide the growth of the canes so that the leaves receive good exposure to the sun; the fruit clusters tend to hang below, ready to drop as the support wires are struck or the vine shaken.

Because grapes are sensitive, the process of mechanical harvesting often results in rupturing the skins of the harvested grapes, making both premature fermentation and unwanted oxidation real possibilities. Since it was impossible to handle the grapes tenderly by machine, and since the fruit had eventually to be crushed, anyway, the inventors hitched up a crushing unit to some models of the harvester and — voilà! — they had a mobile field harvester-crusher.

Not surprisingly, the arrival of the machine in the vineyard was regarded as a mixed blessing. Although the harvest hands knew that picking grapes could be very hard work, some of them didn't cheer the arrival of the mechanical substitute, and in a number of cases, farm labor unions were even able to negotiate contracts that temporarily outlawed the harvester while increasing hourly wages.

Foreign Slopes

If you let your gaze travel across the entire stage of viticulture, you can even today see about five hundred years of vineyard technology represented in the practices of the farmers. In places around the world where labor is cheap and there is either no incentive for progress or capital to finance it, vineyards seem primitive indeed. In parts of Europe and Africa, cultivation and harvesting methods haven't changed in hundreds of years; it's strictly a matter of manpower, muscle, and endurance. There are still steep vineyards along the Moselle and Rhine rivers and in Italy, Spain, and Portugal where

Il Sol è in Libra e il Villanel non teme
L'ire di fosco Ciel grandini e tuoni

SETTEMBRE

Mentre maturi già di Bacco i doni
Joglie alle viti ed in liquor li spreme.

In this mid-eighteenth-century hand-colored line engraving by Francesco Bartolozzi (after Guiseppe Zocchi) entitled Settembre, *grapes are being harvested from tree-climbing vines in the Venetian countryside.* The Christian Brothers Collection.

In this modern, Romanesque-style, stained glass painting by Belgian artist, Michele Broeders, a vintager is shown picking grapes. 17″ square. The Christian Brothers Collection.

A Winzerin, *or vintager woman, harvests grapes from an arbor in this early-twentieth-century color lithograph by Austrian, Ferdinand Andri.*
The Christian Brothers Collection.

Der Herbst. Reg: Fol: N⁰ 8 Autumnus.

some of the harvesters carry small baskets, fill them with grapes from the vines, and grope their way to the ends of those narrow alleys between the vines to dump their cargo into the shoulder pack of a husky co-worker. He in turn must then lug the fruit up or down the hill to the nearest road, where a cart with a big cask waits to take the grapes to the winery.

In other areas, such as California's north-coast premium vineyards you'll find that the basket

Titled Der Herbst, Autumn, *this mid-eighteenth-century line engraving by Johann Friedrich Probst (after a painting by Antoine Watteau), lauds the sweet juice of the grape as the best of autumn's gifts because it gives courage to the young and strength to the old.* The Christian Brothers Collection.

Der Winker.

Macht euch zum Grab geschickt, eh euch der Tod abpflückt.

Die Zeit legt zu des Wintzers Füssen
    der Safft-gefüllten Trauben Pracht;
    und stoltze Schönheit die heut lacht,
wird morgen in die Kelter müssen,
wo Schmertz und Tod die Krafft austreibet,
daß nur die leere Hülse bleibet.

has been replaced by a metal container — far more hygienic because the containers can be steam-cleaned at the end of the day in preparation for the next day's labors. Each member of the harvesting crew dumps the filled containers into a larger one at the end of the alley, and a trailer truck picks up the large container and hauls it off to the winery. Still more advanced is the practice of sending a flatbed trailer with the large container down the alley with the pickers, so that they need not interrupt their work to carry their grapes to the container.

The contrast between the manual operations employed in many of the smaller premium-varietal grape vineyards and the impersonal and swift efficiency of the mechanical harvester evident in the big mass-production vineyards is striking. Both approaches have their place in today's viticultural picture.

Opposite
This etched illustration from Christoph Weigel's Abraham a Sancta Clara, *Nuremberg, 1699, bears the following caption and poem (translation):*
The Vintner
Prepare for the grave before death plucks you down.
Time places at the vintner's feet the glamor of luscious grapes; proud beauty smiles today.
Tomorrow it goes into the press where pain and death drive out all strength and only the empty shell remains.
The Christian Brothers Collection.

Consumer Taste Changing

The harvesting machine and its related devices will find wider use in the years ahead for another reason, and this an esoteric one — consumer taste. It's almost too well known to bear repetition here that since World War II, American consumers have shown a steadily increasing preference for dinner wines, whether red or white, usually on the dry side, but certainly milder in their alcoholic content than the richer dessert wines like sherries and ports. In this respect, they are expressing a preference long accepted in Europe. The table wines range up to about 12 percent alcohol, compared with perhaps 20 percent in dessert wines.

Not to encumber this too much with statistics, it's still important to note that in the fifteen-year span from 1963 through 1978, while Americans were more than doubling their use of wine, table wine usage increased about five-fold, while dessert wines declined in popularity by about two-fifths. The light dinner wines outsold dessert wines about eight-to-one in 1978, and at this writing, they are still increasing in popularity. This has encouraged the planting of thousands of additional acres of wine grapes in California and other states.

This drastic and continuing shift in consumer preference has provided a Roman holiday for marketing analysts. Even more has it paved a golden highway for manufacturers and suppliers of vineyard and winery apparatus, including the mechanical harvester. For, as consumer tastes shifted from sweet to dry wines, the vintner who valued his business had to revise his product mix to increase the emphasis on dinner wines, and either slow up on the sherries and ports or at least level out his production. Moreover, to accommodate the change in taste, the vintner and the growers who supply him with added grapes had to phase out some of the vines that produce grapes for appetizer and dessert wines and replace them with vines producing table-wine grapes.

PALA MISSION.

RUIN SAN LUIS REY.

AN INDIAN CHURCH ORCHESTRA.

ORANGE ORCHARD IN SOUTHERN CALIFORNIA.

P. FRENZENY. THE LAST OF THE FRANCISCANOS.

MAKING WINE.

HERDING HOGS.

SKETCHES IN SOUTHERN CALIFORNIA.—[Drawn by P. Frenzeny.]

New Grape Varieties

So much attention has been focused on the premium-priced varietals — Cabernet Sauvignon, Pinot Noir, and Pinot Chardonnay, to mention the most prominent — that people who enjoy wines have lost sight of an aspect of viticulture that makes a revolving stage of their market resources. This is the work in crossbreeding of grape varieties that's been going on for years at the University of California's Davis campus under the direction of Dr. Harold P. Olmo. It's slow work because vines don't grow overnight, and when the hybrids do yield their fruit, there are still years to wait until they can be planted on a commercial scale, brought to harvest, and the wines made from them evaluated. On the occasions when Dr. Olmo and his colleagues do come up with a successful new grape variety after many failures, they count on a cycle of seventeen to twenty-five years from their initial efforts to bottled commercial product.

At any given time, the Davis viticulturists and enologists may have anywhere from fifty to a hundred crossbreeding experiments at various stages of progress. The qualities they're attempting to breed into their vines are precisely those a vintner would see as ideal if he could somehow manufacture his own grapes.

The researchers are looking, of course, for a grape that will make good wine, and you can write your own definition of that. In addition, they seek a vine that will yield an optimum tonnage of grapes per acre, that will adapt readily to the soil and climate for which it's intended, and that will be resistant to fungi, nematodes, and some of the other calamities to which grapevines fall prey. Quite a goal.

Two splendid examples of the crossbreeding skills of the university's scientists are the Emerald Riesling and the Ruby Cabernet grapes, both of them now enjoying a rising tide of acceptance for blending and even for varietal dinner wines. The first grafts of these varieties were planted in the school's experimental vineyards in the period between 1935 and 1937; thirteen years later, 1948 to 1950, the first commercial plantings of the new hybrids were made, primarily in California's hot Central Valley. It took another four years for the vines to bear and yet more time for the wines to age.

The Emerald Riesling is a white grape that combines the celebrated virtues of the White (Johannisberg) Riesling, pride of the Rhineland, with the Muscadelle du Bordelais from the southwest of France. As its name implies, the Ruby Cabernet is a red grape (actually vintners classify as "black" all grapes that yield red wine). It is a cross between the famous Cabernet Sauvignon and the vigorous Carignane.

Depend on Growers

Almost no vintner with national distribution — certainly none of the major producers — grows all his own grapes. Many wineries maintain extensive acreage in vines, some even supporting nurseries to propagate their own rooted cuttings, but most of them rely on independent growers to supply the bulk of the grapes they require. In California alone, there are more than ten thousand such viticultural entrepreneurs,

Opposite
Harper's Weekly of May, 1878, published this wood engraving made after a drawing by the French artist Paul Frenzeny depicting scenes from southern California. The circular picture at the bottom shows that in early California winemaking, grapes were still crushed with bare feet. After Mexico secularized the missions in 1832, winegrowing became commercialized. The Christian Brothers Collection.

— Ils mettent leurs pieds dedans! mais le vin n'aime pas cela!
— Tu crois?
— Dam! s'il aimait les pieds il ne monterait pas à la tête!

Opposite
Actualites 343: — Ils mettent leurs pieds dedans! mais
le vin n'aime pas cela! — Tu crois. — Dam! s'il aimait
les pieds il ne monterait pas á la tête! (*Actualities
343: They put their feet in there! but the wine
doesn't like that! — You think so? — Madam! if it
liked feet, it wouldn't go to the head!*)
*Cham, the late-nineteenth-century cartoonist for
Charivari, satirizes the stomping of the grapes at
vintage time in this lithograph.* The Christian
Brothers Collection.

*Bunches of wine grapes are about to be caught by the
spiraling blades of a modern crusher.* Photo courtesy
The Wine Institute, San Francisco.

grape growers whose vineyards range in size
from very small to quite large — a very broad
spectrum. Some of these growers sell on the
open market, others contract in advance to sell
their grapes to a specific winery. Still others,
members of a growers' cooperative, depend on
the co-op to find the best market for their fruit,
while a fourth group are members of a co-op
that crushes the grapes and makes and markets
the wine.

Unless contractually prearranged, grape
prices are subject to negotiation at harvest time,
and they reflect the inexorable laws of supply and
demand. If adverse growing conditions have reduced the yield, the market price for a ton of
grapes can be expected to rise; if conditions have

been ideal and the harvest bountiful, prices will likely be soft. Depending on the supply-demand ratio, the swing from year to year can be drastic; for the grower, the price level can be the guide by which the expansion-minded vineyardist decides how much planting of which varieties he will undertake next spring.

It's self-evident that there is — and must be — a direct relationship between the vintner's cost for the grapes and the price tag he puts on a bottle of wine. Fortunately for the consumer, the price spread between California's standard- and premium-quality wines is nowhere near as great as the spread in grape prices. In recent years, a seven-to-one ratio in grape prices was not uncommon— say $150 a ton for an abundant variety, $1000 for a rarer, premium-quality grape. For the wines from those two types of grapes, however, the retail price ratio would probably be no greater than four-to-one.

Best Areas Rare

The difference in quality and price of both grape and wine is not too surprising when you consider the elements involved. Growing the fine grape varieties that develop full flavor and aroma for premium table wines calls for the cooler climates, where the growing season is long and languid and the water — rain plus light sprinkling as needed — is supplied in just the right amount.

These fine varieties produce only two to five tons per acre, and you find them very sparingly around the world: on the rolling hillsides of California's Napa Valley; in certain parts of Burgundy, the vicinity of Beaune, in the Médoc region of Bordeaux; in certain parts of the Moselle Valley and the Middle Rhine; and in Italy in the Chianti Classico region and an area halfway down the "boot" and west of Florence. The grapes, of course, do not develop the same flavor characteristics when grown in the hot Central Valley of California or on some of the plains of southern France, Spain, or North Africa. In the greater heat of these areas, the vines receive much more irrigation, mature one to two months earlier, and yield considerably larger tonnages of grapes per acre.

This miniature wine press of poplar wood was used in the middle of the nineteenth century in the Wachau region of Austria for sample pressings to determine the grapes' sugar content prior to the harvesting. 25½" high. The Christian Brothers Collection.

Opposite
California winery workers during a lunch break about 1910. The apprentice with the refractometer, used to measure the sugar content of the wine, is Ernest Wente of Wente Brothers. Photo courtesy of Wente Brothers.

The Vintage in California — at Work at the Wine Presses, *a hand-colored wood engraving after a drawing by Paul Frenzeny, was published in the October 5, 1878, issue of* Harper's Weekly. *The bustling activity of the harvest is vividly portrayed, with the Chinese laborers playing a vital part in bringing the grape-laden baskets from the fields and unloading them from the wagons, and in the actual crushing of them. The pumps and hoses at lower right are used to transfer the must into the fermenting vats.* The Christian Brothers Collection.

Growing numbers of wine hobbyists have a lot of fun in making their own wine—within the federal limitation of two hundred gallons per family per year. Of course, not many of us are prepared to cope with the twenty-three hundred pounds of grapes (more or less) that it would take to make two hundred gallons of wine. Sensing this, some vintners have developed a tidy business in selling grape juice concentrate which the home winemaker can ferment for his own label after he reconstitutes it with a suitable amount of water. Whether he presses the grapes or chooses the concentrated juice, the weekend vintner is said to account for ten million gallons of wine each year.

The winemaking hobby may become quite expensive for the perfectionist who uses modern equipment for crushing, pressing, fermenting, laboratory testing, and subsequent aging in wood or glass containers. Even with less sophisticated installations and perhaps less perfection in the end product, however, the home winemaker always takes great pride in "his own" creation.

A vintner is shown carrying wine jugs in this anonymous early-sixteenth-century Swiss or German bistre pen and watercolor drawing. The Christian Brothers Collection.

5 The Vintner

For ten or eleven months of the year, a winery is a delightfully restful place to be. It's usually far enough from city noise to seem somnolent. The cavernous fermentation rooms and storage areas are dark and cool and silent; and the persistent fragrance of past vintages permeates a winery as distinctively as the bouquet of burnt incense and beeswax candles invests an ancient cathedral. Except for the occasional distant clatter of bottling, labeling, and casing machines and the whirr of forklifts at the loading dock, a winery during this period creates the illusion of time at rest.

From the day the first grape is harvested, though, the winery is transformed; and until the last grape is picked and crushed and fermented, it is a busy, busy place of seven-day weeks in which the conventional forty-hour stint is just a warm-up. The activity is most striking at a very large winery, where for days on end there's a continuous stream of large gondola-bed trucks heaped high with grapes: purples and reds and greens and yellows. The gondolas dump their cargo directly into a screw conveyor feeding the crusher, then the trucks head back to the vineyard for a fresh load.

Besides being a busy time, it is also a critical period for the winery and its cellarmaster, as well as for the people who staff the quality-control laboratory, keep the machines humming, and above all preserve a high level of hygiene to protect the precious juices against bacteria and stray cells of unwanted yeast. Contrary to popular belief, even the fermented wine doesn't have enough alcoholic wallop to resist bacterial attack. If the winery is to realize the best possible results for its efforts, then the labors of all these functionaries must be mobilized and synchronized in the two fast-moving months that follow the harvest.

Whether it's a large or a small winery, when the vintage begins, a great number of activities start happening, all at the same time. So it might be useful here to examine these virtually simultaneous processes one by one to see how they converge to produce a bottle of wine for our dinner table.

A good place to start is with the confusion that surrounds the terms, "crushing" and "pressing." Why, one may wonder, is it necessary to both crush and press? Don't both processes squeeze the juice out of the grape?

Processes Differ

Crushing and pressing are two distinct and necessary functions, and they are not employed in the same way for white wines as for red.

Action at the winery begins when a load of grapes is dumped into a conveyor leading to a crusher. Despite its name, the crusher, which is usually located outdoors, is not a grape smasher in the sense of a hammermill or in the picture-esque sense of a host of *pisadors* tramping out the juice with their special nail-studded shoes. The crusher does two things for both the white and the black grapes: It gently sweeps the berries from the stems and in the process ruptures the grape skins, permitting some freed juice to run off and be transferred immediately to a fermenting tank. At the same time, it ejects the

Under the heading Vignerons *an early-nineteenth-century French artist portrayed in five hand-colored engravings winemaking in France: pruning the vines, harvesting the grapes, crushing, pressing, and* bottling. The Christian Brothers Collection.

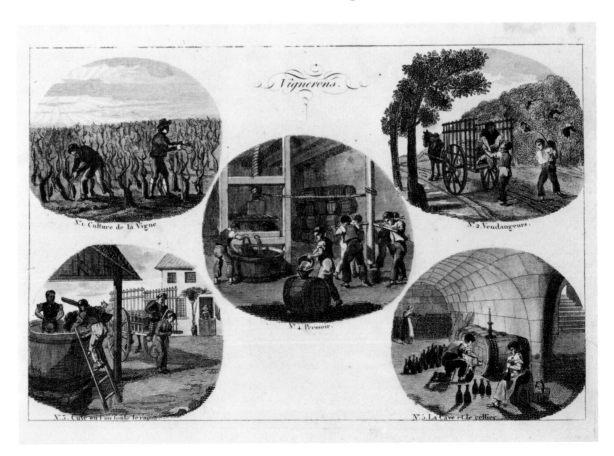

In many family-operated wineries, the wife and children had to help the vintner at harvest time. Here in this late-nineteenth-century etching by Ferdinand Schmutzer, an Austrian peasant couple are shown working a wine press. The Christian Brothers Collection.

skeletal stems, which are then disposed of as waste. Not surprisingly, the juice obtained in the manner described above is called "free run," since it is obtained without supplemental squeezing or pressing.

In the premium-quality wine operation, the white and the black grapes are crushed separately, often by means of different crushing units, and the loads are segregated by varieties. No Gamay grapes, for example, would be permitted to go into a crusher processing Barberas; and with the whites, no Sémillon would be permitted where Johannisberg Riesling is being crushed.

With the free-run juice taken care of and the stems ejected, the remaining mixture of skins, grape pulp, and seeds, which is called "must," * now flows from the crusher, and here the paths of what is to be red wine and what is to be white diverge.

Fermenting Red Wine

From the crusher, the red wine must is pumped to a fermentation tank, which can be made of wood or of stainless steel, holds thousands of gallons, and is open at the top. The

---

* From the Latin *vinum mustum*, meaning "new wine."

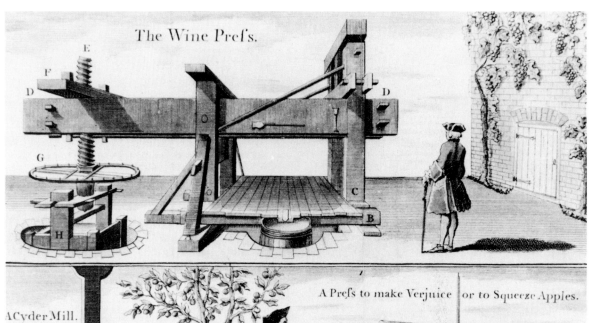

The Wine Prefs.

A Cyder Mill.

A Prefs to make Verjuice or to Squeeze Apples.

Printed for J. Hinton at the Kings Arms St Pauls Church Yard. 1717.

wild yeasts that grow on the grape skins are neutralized and a special strain of vintner's pure yeast is added. Before long, the yeast begins to transform the grape sugar into equal parts of alcohol and carbon-dioxide gas. The liquid mixture begins to bubble and hiss from the escaping carbon dioxide and continues to do so throughout its period of fermentation, which can last from several days to several weeks, depending on a number of factors, including temperature. Fermentation creates heat and it is good winery practice to keep the temperature within bounds by means of cooling devices. Cool, slow fermentation helps preserve the aroma and flavor of the grape in the wine being created.

Fermentation is complete when the hissing and bubbling stop. The tank now contains red wine of about 12 percent alcohol resting above a layer of grape pulp, seeds, and skins. (The rich color of the wine comes from the insides of the skins, and red wines are therefore said to have been fermented "on the skins.")

From the fermenting tank, the wine is now transferred to holding tanks and subsequently to aging casks where it starts the long, mysterious process by which a good red wine acquires dignity and maturity.

In this anonymous English hand-colored line engraving dated 1747, a wine press and a cider mill are pictured. The wine press was designed to produce a great amount of pressure. The juice, or must, was collected in casks below ground level and then transferred from there to the fermenting vats. The Christian Brothers Collection.

This late-eighteenth-century etching depicts a German artist's conception of an early pot-still. The wine is heated and evaporated in the closed pot on the open fire, piped into the larger cask where it is condensed, and then the distillate runs into the smaller cask. The Christian Brothers Collection.

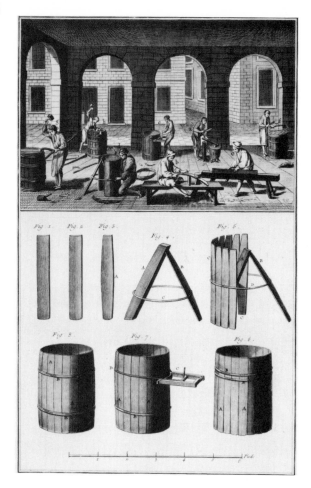

The important and highly-skilled art of the cooper
is represented here in this hand-colored line
engraving by Robert Bénard from Denis Diederot's
Encyclopedia, *published in Paris in 1762.*
The Christian Brothers Collection.

The cooper is the subject of this mid-sixteenth-
century woodcut by Jost Amman. Since the Middle
Ages and into the twentieth century, casks were
made by hand. Coopers not only made casks, but also
took care of their maintenance and repair. Many
aging casks bear the mark of their maker and often
last more than a hundred years. The Christian
Brothers Collection.

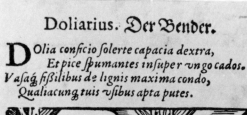

Doliarius. Der Bender.

Dolia conficio folerte capacia dextra,
  Et pice fpumantes infuper vngo cados.
Vafaq fiffilibus de lignis maxima condo,
  Qualiacung tuis vfibus apta putes.

Autumnus preffis vbi largior imminet vuis,
  Atq mero Bacchus fpumat vbiq nouo,
Rufticus huc veniat calcatis fordidus vuis,
  Et plauftro coëmat lignea vafa fuo.
Dolia fanari quoq curet agentia rimas,
  Ne vetulos rumpant feruida mufta cados.

L 3   Arcu-

The liquid-like must left in the fermenting tank is pumped to a press. Here, direct force squeezes out much of the remaining wine; this in turn is moved into a tank for aging. The mass of dry skins, pulp, and seeds left in the press, which is known as "pomace," can either be modified into a nutritious cattle feed or be returned to the vineyard soil as an organic fertilizer.

Let's back up momentarily. Suppose the cellarmaster has decided that this batch — maybe they're Grenache grapes — will make a pleasant rosé wine. After a few days of fermentation "on the skins," when he has determined that the must has just the right blush of pink, he removes the skins and allows fermentation to proceed without them. Rosé wine offers us the clearest possible demonstration of how a wine

This early-nineteenth-century color aquatint by John Hill (after a drawing by John Claude Nattes), Les Bains de Julien, Paris, shows the interior of a cooperage shop in Paris. In order to bend the wooden staves into the required shape, the cooper in the center heats the unfinished barrel over an open fire. The Christian Brothers Collection.

derives its pigmentation from the skins. A more dramatic example is the occasional use of red grapes to make white wine and the removal of the skins before fermentation commences.

Making White Wines

Back to the crusher now to follow the white grapes, which are actually closer to greens and yellows. Instead of being steered into the fermenter from the crusher, the white grapes go directly to the press, where the juice is squeezed out. The pomace is removed and the pure juice, with the appropriate dollop of yeast, goes to the fermenter where the natural sugar starts to break down into alcohol and carbon dioxide.

White wines are inherently more delicate than reds, and this quality makes its presence felt in the processing, in the storability, and in the serving. Immediate extraction of the juice and separation from the skins is but the first step in the very special care the winemaker gives his whites. The reader may have already sensed his second move: reduction of the fermentation temperature. When the grapes are delivered to the crusher, they can be at a temperature anywhere from seventy to one hundred degrees Fahrenheit in the north-coastal valleys of California that are noted for the elegance of their white wines. Fermented in that temperature range, the grapes would exhaust their sugars in a few days and the resulting wine would lack the anticipated subtle flavor and aroma characteristics. To prevent this, to stretch out the fermentation process and thereby allow the wines to achieve their full potential at their own pace, the proficient vintner has jacketed the fermenters with an outer wall in which a coolant circulates to hold temperatures down to between thirty-five and fifty degrees Fahrenheit. Some wineries, indeed, ferment white wines in air-conditioned rooms.

Not all white wines are fermented to the total conversion of their sugars. For subtle flavor differences, especially in some of the rarer varietal wines, a resourceful vintner may interrupt the fermentation of, say, a vat of Chénin Blanc juice before all the sugar has become alcohol. The residual sugar then imparts a delicate sweetness to the wine that results, lifting it out of the slightly astringent class of a "bone-dry" wine.

California law prohibits the addition of cane or beet sugar — or any sweetening other than natural grape sugar — in the making of a table or dessert wine. This can be done legally outside California and in certain European countries where the grapes, lacking sun, often don't reach the required sugar level on their own.* Because of this stringent California law, which was instituted at the behest of the vintners themselves, any sweetness you detect in a California table or dessert wine is always the natural sugar from the grapes.

Aging Begins

With completion of fermentation, both the red wines and the whites are ready for aging. First, however, they are drawn off to holding tanks for a rest of a few weeks to a few months. While they're resting in these large wood or stainless-steel vessels, microscopic particles of sediment called "lees" settle to the bottom. In a large winemaking operation, the lees accumulate in quantities large enough to justify putting them aside for sale as a byproduct; the red-wine lees contain tannin, among other things, which is used to color-stamp meat.

Ready for aging, the reds and the whites again follow different paths. White wines, broadly speaking, do not improve with long aging; they're better when drunk fairly young; also they're much more susceptible to oxidation than red wines. It's a sad experience to put away a pleasant dry white dinner wine for a special occasion and then, when you're ready to serve it, discover that it has the telltale brownish cast of oxidation. However, some whites — the sweeter Rhines, Moselles, and Sauternes, for example — may take two to four years to reach their full maturity.

---

* It may be noted in passing that the evolution of the European Economic Community has now tightened certain regulations pertaining to the addition of non-grape sugar to must or wine by obliging member countries to harmonize their rules on winemaking and labeling.

Coopers of each winegrowing region developed their own characteristic shapes and sizes of casks. In this etching dated 1770 by Jean Jacques de Boissieu, a rigid cylindrical-shaped cask is being produced. The Christian Brothers Collection.

The cooper's trade, a dying art, was still practiced in the mid-1950s by Hans Hoffmann in the Napa Valley in California. On his schnitzelbank work bench, he shaves a barrel stave in order to repair a cask.

WINE VAULT, ANAHEIM, INTERIOR.

WINE VAULT, ANAHEIM, EXTERIOR.

WINE CELLARS AND RESIDENCE OF **F.A.KORN.** ANAHEIM, LOS ANGELES CO., CAL.

The wine cellars and residence of F. A. Korn are the subject of this hand-colored reproduction lithograph from the History of Los Angeles County, California *published by Thompson & West in 1880. The interior and exterior of the "wine vault," built of solid brick for optimum temperature control and stability in the above-ground "cellar," are shown in the upper register.* The Christian Brothers Collection.

Most of the whites, then, can be transferred from the holding tanks to storage casks and eventually to the bottling line, where the bottles are filled, corked, labeled, and cased; they will be ready for the market within a short time. The especially promising ones will be kept in aging vessels of wood or stainless steel, or in glass-lined tanks until the cellarmaster and his fellow tasters are satisfied that the wines are ready to be bottled. There are some fine white wines where additional bottle aging will further enhance the quality (up to a point) but, in general, white and rosé wines should be drunk while they're fairly young—say up to three years of age.

To Smaller Casks

Red wines, on the other hand, possess an inherent capacity to improve with age. This is especially true of premium wines produced

Rows of oaken aging vats are shown in The Christian Brothers' Greystone winery at St. Helena, Napa Valley. When a vat is empty, the door at the bottom is opened so that a worker may enter the vat and thoroughly clean it.

from grapes of high quality — for example, the Gamay Noir, the Pinot Noir, and the Cabernet Sauvignon, or for any of the reds that wind up on the dealer's shelf behind a varietal label. However, they don't all have the same aging characteristics, and here is where the skill of the winemaker comes into play, for he must know when a fine red wine has reached its peak in the wooden cask and the time has come to bottle it. Until that time, the vinification process, the art of the premium quality winemaker, calls for the wines to be "racked," or transferred from the larger redwood or oak casks to successively smaller oak casks holding fifty to sixty gallons. In the process of transfer, of course, the aging wine is separated from its sediment, or lees. It's said that the smaller cask ages the wine more effectively because it increases the ratio of wood surface to wine volume.

Varietal table wines aging in an old California north-coast winery. Oak casks originally came from Europe, and sometimes the barrelheads were decoratively carved. The one pictured commemorates this nation's centennial.

Exactly what goes on in those aromatic casks has never been fully determined, and the change that occurs in the wine is not one that can be fully detected by chemical analysis. It's assumed that some interchange with air is involved since wines age better in wooden casks than in stainless-steel tanks. The wine permeates the wood and actually evaporates, as much as 2 to 5 percent a year. The small pocket of air left in the cask by evaporation must be displaced with wine or it will oxidize the cask's contents. This is called "topping," an operation that's performed every week in those wineries that produce the best wines; an attendant adds enough wine from a similar batch to displace the air pocket.

With the evaporation loss so great, it's important that the topping wine be of the same quality as that in the cask, and a little simple arithmetic will show why this is so. If the wine is aged for a number of years, the volume loss could add up to as much as 20 percent. To justify that kind of irretrievable loss, the wine must be of fine quality.

It has already been noted that racking, besides transferring the aging premium wine to smaller and smaller casks, serves an additional purpose. As the wine matures, it throws off a certain amount of sediment that eventually settles at the bottom of the cask. The sediment, or lees, could be filtered out every time. But each filtration would rob delicate wines of some of their aroma and flavor elements, while racking does not. In racking, the wine is drawn off through hoses or transparent tubes without disturbing the sediment, which is then filtered out of the remaining few gallons.

It is the duty of the cellarmaster to decide when any given cask is ready for racking, and also when it's ready for bottling. He does this by tasting and sniffing the contents of each cask at regular intervals, studying its color and clarity, and jotting down his observations in a record book. Almost never, though, does he depend solely on his own judgment that a wine is ready to be bottled. He assembles a panel of several experts from the people around him to taste and judge the contents of one or more, usually several, casks. The tasters compare notes, and if they disagree on a wine, they may try it again. The object is to arrive at a consensus and not depend on any single palate or nose or eye to pronounce final judgment. Usually, the panelists will also decide at this point whether the wine is to be bottled as is or to be blended with one or more different wines before going to market.

Blend or Vintage

A good deal of dust has been stirred up over the years around the question of whether it's more desirable to blend wines for the sake of high quality and uniformity, or to bottle them under a vintage label as they come from the aging casks. It isn't so much a disagreement as it is a consumer misunderstanding of the origin, scope, and semantics of the word *vintage*.

In France, which has been the shrine of many who possess a sense of discrimination in the choice of exquisite wines, and in Germany, Switzerland, Austria, and northern Italy, vineyards are not blessed by climatic uniformity. One year brings enough sunshine to permit the grapes to reach full maturity. When that happens, there's no need to add sugar during fermentation, and the winemaker has within his grasp a wine he can boast about. Another year, the sun is less benevolent. Over an average ten-year span in most European wine areas, a vintner can count on two superb vintages and perhaps two good vintages. Since these are better wines, he is justified in demanding a higher price for them and in identifying the high-priced wine with a vintage-year label. The other six years? It's been remarked that the people in Bordeaux have never seen the Garonne River running red from wine that failed to meet vintage standards.

Winegrowing areas in the United States don't have that climate problem. Grapes almost always mature on the vine, so the addition of sugar during fermentation is a rarity; in California, as noted before, it's against the law in the making of table and dessert wines. Consequently climate is not one of the critical variables that account for the difference between, say, a 1965 and a 1966 California Pinot Noir. The difference is there, of course, because never in nature have there been two grape harvests exactly alike. But it is not because the grapes may not have reached maturity one of those years.

Some American vintners, adopting the European custom, are loyal adherents of vintage labeling. They conform to the rigid U.S. laws that require 95 percent of a vintage-labeled wine to consist of wine of the designated year that originated in the general growing area specified on the label. (Five percent leeway is allowed for topping.)

Comparative tasting is a highly productive exercise for those aficionados who enjoy spotting the differences in a wine from one vintage year to another. It accounts for much of the pleasure they experience from drinking wine.

For the multitude who prefer to choose wines they know beforehand they'll enjoy, the practice among vintners is to blend wines of a given type to optimum quality and to a predetermined taste standard. This enables the retail customer to buy, say, a Johannisberg Riesling or a Cabernet Sauvignon of a given brand with the assurance that it will taste exactly like the Johannisberg Riesling or Cabernet Sauvignon of the same brand he enjoyed last week.

The Vintner's Art

In the entire winemaking process, no single step imposes such a heavy burden on the skill of the cellarmaster as the blending of quality wines. This is truly the essence of the vintner's art. Among its most dedicated practitioners are The Christian Brothers of Mont La Salle Vineyards in the Napa Valley of California. It has been their experience that with the exception of some occasional outstanding vintage bottlings, it is precision blending that enhances the fine quality of a wine. They have learned it is often possible to give a younger wine more depth of taste by the addition of a small quantity of an older wine; and, on the other hand, to provide an older wine with an extra touch of life by blending in some of a younger.

When this is done skillfully, blending assures the consumer of a consistency of high quality and continuity of taste and aroma in the wines he buys from week to week and year to year, and the Sauvignon Blanc of a given brand purchased in San Francisco this week will taste approximately the same as the one purchased in New York the week before.

How is it done? Different wineries may differ somewhat in method, but the practice won't deviate too much from the blending session that convened on July 16, 1979 at Mont La Salle Vineyards in California's Napa Valley. On the panel of experts assembled by Brother Timothy, F.S.C., cellarmaster of The Christian Brothers wines, were David Cofran, the Mont La Salle enologist and John Hoffman, vice-president and production manager at Mont La Salle. Members of the panel were chosen not so much because of their titles or occupations but because each is a well-qualified and experienced wine taster.

Choosing the Blend

The panel's mission was to choose a blend of Cabernet Sauvignon wines to be bottled in the last half of 1979 for release to the market not earlier than the last half of 1980. The "raw" material they had to work with was The Brothers' entire inventory of Cabernet Sauvignon wine — 1976 and older, including different vintages from different vineyard locations. There was assembled

Opposite
In the Bouchonnier, *a line engraving by Robert Benard from Diderot's* Encyclopedia *of 1762, corkmakers are shown carefully cutting bottle corks from the cork-oak bark* (Quercus suber). The Christian Brothers Collection.

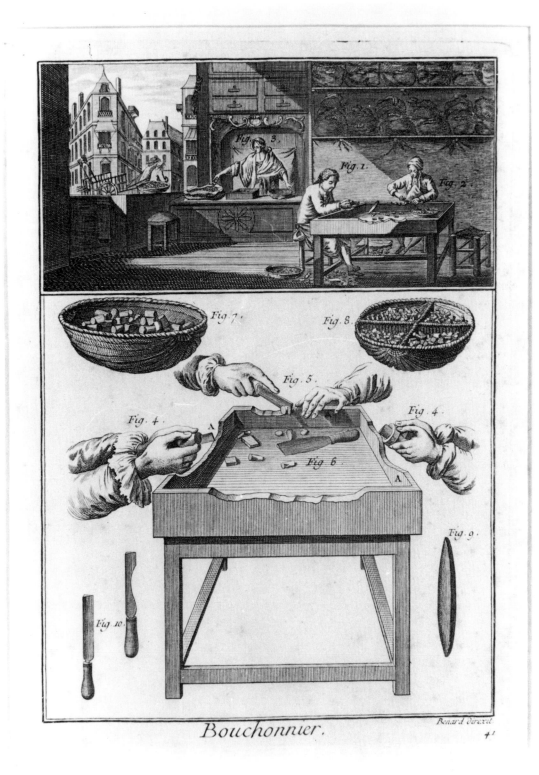

Bouchonnier.

Benard direxit.

before the panel a bottle of wine, identified only by number, from each of 95 oak casks or redwood wine tanks. In front of each bottle stood a wineglass washed in pure water, hung upside down to drip-dry, then sloshed with a little wine to eliminate any unwanted odors. An ounce or two from its mating bottle was poured into each glass.

Then the panel began the tasting, an unhurried process that was to last several days. Each of the panelists viewed, smelled, and tasted the many separate wines and jotted down his impressions. It now became David Cofran's job to begin the blending experiments. From one bottle he took a few measured drops of wine in a graduated pipette and allowed them to dribble into a glass, each two centiliters being proportional to a thousand gallons of wine. To the glass he added fifteen centiliters

The wine taster in this seventeenth-century Dutch engraved illustration draws a sample into the shallow tasting cup by opening a small hole in the cask. He will then close the hole by inserting a wooden peg. The Christian Brothers Collection.

from another bottle, five from another. When he finished that blend, he noted the proportions carefully on his record and started another. As each was completed, the judges repeated the ritual of examination—looking, sniffing, and sipping.

In the five days it took to reach a decision, David Cofran and Brother Timothy concocted eight different blends using different quantities of Cabernet Sauvignon from the several vintages and locations. If they seemed unduly deliberative, their caution was understandable; the droplets they were sniffing and tasting and viewing in the light would narrow down to a single blend and would, in the volume they contemplated, repre-

Aging wine has to be checked at regular intervals. To take a sample from a cask, the vintner can draw some wine from the bung hole on top or drill a small hole on the side, which is then closed with short wooden plugs, as is shown in this seventeenth-century German woodcut book illustration. The Christian Brothers Collection.

158

This eighteenth-century Austrian polychromed wood figurine depicts a vintager holding up a bunch of grapes while carrying a small barrel under his arm. 7½" high. The Christian Brothers Collection.

sent more than one-half year's bottling of Cabernet Sauvignon.

Components of Blend

In the end, the blend they chose as most closely matching The Christian Brothers' characteristic taste for Napa Valley Cabernet Sauvignon wine was made up of four successive vintages, as follows:

1971	6%
1974	22%
1975	49.5%
1976	22.5%

The four selected wines were drawn from 33 different aging casks of European and American oak, and 6 redwood wine aging tanks. In the aggregate, 100 percent of the wines were from Cabernet Sauvignon grapes, far above the legal minimum requirement of the grape variety that is to give the wine its name. A part of the grapes that went into the blend were grown by The Brothers, the other bought from independent growers under contract with The Brothers.

After the blend was chosen, the pipette measurements were scaled up to the hundreds and thousands of gallons, the wines were commingled in a great vat, and the blend was allowed to rest for more than three months. Then, after another careful taste check, the 79,306 gallons were bottled and stored away for twelve months. If the blending panel's skills lived up to promise, that bottling will be hardly distinguishable in taste, aroma, and visual delight from the previous bottling.

Diverse Cooperage

It must be evident from the discussion of crushing, pressing, holding, aging, racking, and blending that a winery's inventory of containers is formidable in variety, in numbers, and in total capacity. This proliferation of cooperage and tankage is brought on, for a California winemaker at least, by the extraordinary range of grape varieties available to him, the need to keep them separated, and the number of stages that each wine must go through before it is bottled.

À BERCY:
— Nous faisons tout ce que nous pouvons pour empêcher que la Seine déborde jamais
et il y a pourtant encore des gens qui ne nous savent pas gré de notre bonne intention !......

It's not uncommon for a winery of only moderate size to crush as many as eighteen or twenty different varieties of grapes and for a larger winery to handle thirty or forty. To be unprepared with appropriate storage is to risk financial loss, as some French vintners learned many years ago when they unexpectedly harvested a bumper crop of grapes. With no room for storing the extra wine, they were obliged to distill it into brandy or accept a major loss.

A visitor to a California premium winery can encounter a bewildering assortment of containers from larger tanks of select redwood or oak containing thousands of gallons down to the small

Actualités 321. À Bercy: — Nous faisons tout ce que nous pouvons pour empêcher que la Seine déborde jamais et il y a pourtant encore des gens qui ne nous savent pas gré de notre bonne intention! . . . (Actualities 321. At Bercy: — *We do everything in our power to make sure that the Seine can never overflow, and yet there are some people who don't appreciate our good intentions.) One of the many satirical cartoon lithographs by Honoré Daumier parodying the winemaker; this one was published in an 1856 edition of* Charivari. The Christian Brothers Collection.

barriques of American or limousin oak holding just shy of sixty gallons and including some handsomely carved casks of usually venerable age. It would probably not occur to him that the care of all these vessels presents unique problems in sanitation and maintenance that are almost as complex as winemaking. Wine people, by the way, use the generic word "casks" to describe their containers; they think of "barrels" as beer containers.

Precisely how the seasoned wood modifies the flavor of a wine is impossible to say, but an experienced taster with a sensitive palate can distinguish between two similar wines that have been aged in different casks. It should be obvious, then, that an important member of the winery staff is the cooper. Basically the cooper fabricates the casks, cutting and fitting the staves and the heads and applying the hoops. Because he is a member of a fast-disappearing craft, some of his work has been taken over by machines — with no noticeable improvement, it may be added.

Maintenance Is Vital

Making casks is only the first requirement of the cooper. He must also supervise the maintenance work of the wine-cellar staff. Casks must be flushed out after each use. Empty casks must be fumigated with burning sulphur to inhibit any bacterial growth. Between uses they must occasionally be filled with water; otherwise the staves dry out and separate. If a cask is not properly cleaned, bacteria may grow inside and between the staves. Then it must be taken apart stave by stave, each stave cleaned, then the cask reassembled. This is strictly the work of the deft cooper. Before he restores the hoops, he also paints their inside surfaces, the sides that touch the cask, to discourage rusting at a place that later will be unreachable.

Casks come in many shapes and sizes, and though they're known by different names in different countries, they have no nationality. The barrique, traditional in Bordeaux and Burgundy, becomes an oxhoft in English-speaking areas; it holds 225 liters, close to 60 gallons, or 300

fifths of wine. From Germany comes the *Stückfässer*, with a capacity of 1,200 liters, and the *Halbstücke*, which oddly accommodates not 600 but 640 liters. Germany also gives us the *Fuder*, containing 960 liters, primarily for Moselle, and the *HalbFuder*. To Spain we are indebted for puncheons (600 liters), and the *bota*, or butt, holding 132 gallons, for sherry in transit; and to Portugal for pipes (522 liters for port wine, 416 liters for Madeira).

You're likely to find any or all of these round- or oval-contoured casks in American wineries producing both premium-quality dinner wines and premium dessert wines such as sherry and port. Some of the casks that trace their ancestry to Europe and perhaps to another century are heavily ornamented with carvings of grapes, cupids, festive *bon vivants*, even religious themes.

By contrast, wineries producing wine in massive volume that will be sold within a year or so have found it advantageous to build up their enormous fermenting and storage capacity in gigantic tanks of concrete, stainless steel, or glass-lined steel. They are expressly in the business of producing wines for the broad and basic market, wines to be sold and drunk while young and priced in reflection of the comparative simplicity of their production and to appeal to modest budgets. These wineries rival in size some of the great industrial corporations, and because of their enormous production and sales volume, are able to mobilize platoons of trained viticulturists, enologists, chemists, and cellar technologists to create wines of agreeable quality and uniformity.

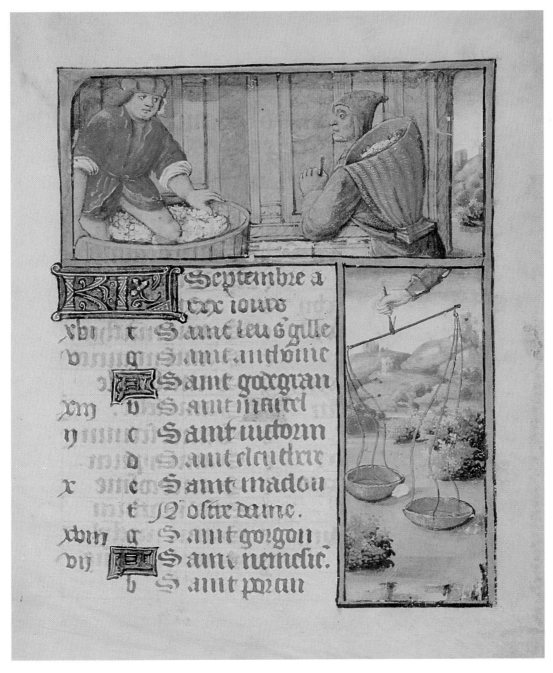

During the late Middle Ages, the most popular devotional books for the laity were the small Books of Hours. The late-fifteenth-century artist of this vellum calendar page painted a simple vintage scene and the scales of Libra as illustrations for the month of September. The Christian Brothers Collection.

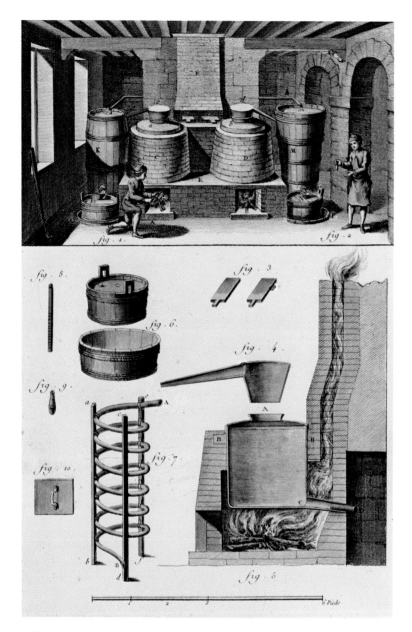

The traditional brandy pot-still, in its primitive eighteenth-century form, is shown in this hand-colored line engraving by Defehrt (after a drawing by Goussier) from Diderot's Encyclopedia, *dated 1762. The spiral pipe is part of the condenser.*
The Christian Brothers Collection.

Opposite
In The Vintage, *a late-eighteenth-century stipple etching by Francesco Bartolozzi (after a painting by David Teniers the Younger), the vintner is shown checking the first pressing of the current harvest.*
The Christian Brothers Collection.

D. Teniers. Pinxt.   F. Bartolozzi Sculp.

THE VINTAGE.

No Bad Wine

Thanks to the aggressive stride of these firms in large-scale vinification, it can be said that practically no bad wine is being produced in the United States today. Some wines, made from inexpensive grapes grown in hot areas under heavy irrigation, perhaps fall short in flavor and aroma, but they're almost always sound wines with a normal shelf life. Since they promise little or no improvement through aging, there's no purpose in keeping them a long time, anyway; they are usually purchased to be used almost immediately.

It needs to be said of these popularly priced wines that because of statutory standards propagated by the wine industry, and because of the modern technology underlying their production, they have achieved and are maintaining a level of purity as high as many imported wines commanding two and three times the price. They throw hardly any sediment, for example, because winemakers have learned how to remove it at the winery. Not too many years ago, even quality wines in Europe could, under aging, throw off a powdery deposit or a film of tannin that coated the inner surface of the bottle. Some carelessly produced wines exported to the United States still show a tendency to throw off sediment after a short time.

It's a point of collateral interest that modern technology has obsoleted the woven basket designed to cradle a wine bottle at the dinner table. It originated as a device to allow sediment to collect where it wouldn't be decanted into the wine glass. Using the basket is a harmless practice, and for some hosts it may seem a graceful touch. But for American wines and many modern European wines, it's no longer necessary except possibly for high-quality wines after many years of bottle aging.

Innovative Wines

Up to this point, the discussion of winemaking has been limited to those wines of moderate alcohol content, the so-called table wines, or dinner wines, in red, pink, and white classifications usually associated with mealtime use. The 7 to

Perkeo, a famous court jester of the eighteenth century at the court of Prince Karl Philip of Heidelberg, was known for his tremendous capacity for wine. An eighteenth-century German woodcarver immortalized him in this small figurine, and shows him carrying a wine barrel on his back. 8" high. The Christian Brothers Collection.

13 percent of alcohol that they contain serves the dual purpose of enhancing our pleasure in their use and protecting the wine, when it's properly stored, against deterioration and spoilage.

Some of the larger and more innovative American winemakers, seeking a product that would appeal to the tastes of younger consumers, experimented with the addition of other natural flavors to their basic table wines. For the innovators, the acceptance of flavored wines by the oncoming generation was a marketing sensation of the sixties and seventies. The sale of the so-called "pop" or "mod" wines reached an equivalent of 14 percent of the United States wine market before the sales dropped off to relative insignificance.

The Brandy Legend

Not all of California's wineries participate in flavored wine ventures, nor do they all put wine through the distillation process that makes it brandy. The figures vary from year to year. In the sixties and seventies, bonded wineries in California ranged between 225 and 375 while those licensed to make or store brandy numbered between 76 and 90.

Anyone who has observed the reverent awe in which some brandy drinkers contemplate a Cognac of special reputation recognizes that distillation is an art. The legend is that brandy originated as a logistic expedient of the sixteenth-century maritime trade between Bordeaux and The Netherlands. Dutch merchants were eager for France's choice wines, but the small ships couldn't accommodate enough casks to satisfy market demand. A sea captain hit upon the stratagem of concentrating the wine by distilling out the water, then reconstituting it with water at destination. The Dutch merchants sampled the distillate, liked it, and sold it as it was. They called it *brandewijn*, meaning "burnt wine," and the word was eventually Anglicized to brandy.

Virtually every place where wine is grown, some of it is distilled into brandy under such distinctive names as Metaxa (Greece), Armagnac (France), and the licorice-flavored ouzo (Greece and Cyprus). Israel even produces a kosher brandy. The French marc and Italian grappa are distilled from pomace.

There are wide variations in quality among the brandies of the world, depending on the variety of grapes used for the basic wine, the method of distillation, and the art of the distiller in cask aging and then blending his beverage brandy. In France, Cognac has no rival in popularity. Spain, too, has a fine reputation for its brandies. In the United States, the California-grown brandy of The Christian Brothers has enjoyed the greatest consumer acceptance for many years.

Dessert Wines

However popular as a beverage, brandy has an additional use. In the production of the so-called "fortified" wines — sherry, port, Madeira, Muscatel, and others in the category of sweet "dessert" wines — a high-proof brandy is added to the must long before fermentation has converted all the grape sugar to alcohol and carbon dioxide. The fortifying brandy differs from beverage brandy in strength; it can be from 145 to 190 proof as compared with about 80 proof for the brandy we drink.

In dessert-wine processing, the brandy serves two purposes. First, it halts fermentation before all the grape sugar is used up, letting the wine retain a certain amount of natural sweetness. Second, it brings the alcohol content up to the 17 to 21 percent range required of all dessert wines. Left alone, the must would probably convert all the grape sugar to alcohol, leaving a dry beverage. So, in his quest for a sweet dessert wine, the winemaker — knowing that fermentation automatically stops when the alcohol content reaches approximately 15 percent — adds brandy at a specific point, generally early in the fermentation, and in this way attains his goal. It's nowhere as simple as that sounds, of course, for the winemaker must fine-tune the process to the exact level of natural sweetness and the precise alcohol content he wishes to achieve; and must then apply all the other proce-

LA BOTTE DÀ DEL VINO, CH' ELL' HÀ.

VINO DI
GIVSEPPE
M.ª MITELLI
1677.

G.M. Mitelli I. e F.

Suol conforme a la causa esser l'effetto,
Ne d'infetto liquor l'urna ripiena
Vale à sominstrar balsamo eletto.

dures of winemaking, including blending and aging the dessert wines that result.

Sparkling Wines

Of all the categories of wines, none is so suggestive of ceremony, festivity, and pageantry as Champagne and the other sparkling wines, like Sparkling Burgundy, Asti Spumante, Sekt, and in recent years Cold Duck. They are the wines that the French, with their restrictive definition of Champagne as the sparkling product of the Champagne District, classify as *vin mousseux*.

The sparkle is imparted by bubbles of carbon dioxide that are generated in a closed vessel by second-stage fermentation of a selected, finished still wine. The fermentation can be induced in a large container, a process known as the Charmat process after its inventor; or in the bottle, the traditional method. In either case, the secondary fermentation is brought on by the addition of sweetening and yeast to a finished still wine. Little additional alcohol is created and the carbon dioxide, developing considerable pressure, is locked into the wine.

Whether the Champagne is produced by the Charmat process or is bottle fermented, the most important factor is the quality of the wines chosen for the *cuvée*, the blend. Second in importance is the use of pure champagne yeast, which reputable producers propagate themselves.

Disgorging Sediment

No matter how clear the *cuvée*, the yeast that's added produces a little sediment that has to be removed. The trick is to get rid of this sediment without sacrificing too much carbon dioxide, which should retain a pressure of about seventy pounds in the bottle. In some champagne cellars using bottle fermentation, the traditional disgorging process is still followed. Sediment settles on the cork because the bottles are placed upside down in racks and given a quarter-turn every week for several weeks. When the sediment has settled, the neck of the bottle is dipped into a quick-freezing bath, the cork is popped and the frozen sediment with it. Any wine that escapes is replaced at this point — before the bottle gets its final closure.

Many modern Champagne producers outside France use the "transfer" method, whereby the Champagne, after the secondary fermentation is complete, is transferred under pressure from the bottles into a large tank. From there, as in the Charmat process, it is sent through a sediment-removing filter to the bottling machine. Before the bottled Champagne is corked, a dollop of sweetened wine is added to relieve the bone-dryness.

The traditional champagne cork, ejected from the bottle, has the shape of a belle in a hoopskirt, and it's a continuing mystery how it can be compressed to be forced into the narrower neck of the bottle. Even with this pressure-defying contour, the cork is held tight to the neck of the bottle with a forcefully twisted wire basket. Less expensive sparkling wines often use a plastic closure, which is also secured with the wire hood. Where the exigencies of hospitality require great numbers of bottles to be opened in a short time without need for the "pop," as in airline service, some Champagne makers allow their wine to leave the cellar under a crown cap. But, just as half the pleasure in a steak is in the sizzle, the festive element in Champagne rests partly in the popping of the cork. It would seem unlikely, therefore, that the traditional cork's future is endangered.

Opposite
The Italian proverb, La botte dà del vino, ch'ell'hà *(The barrel yields as much wine as it has), is the subject of this 1677 etching by Giuseppe Maria Mitelli. The Christian Brothers Collection.*

California's Versatility

European visitors never cease to be astonished by the product versatility of American wineries. How is it possible, they ask, that a winery in

166

California can offer so many different categories of wine when in Bordeaux a vintner makes only Bordeaux (claret), in Burgundy only Burgundy, and on the Rhine only Rhine wine? What accounts for the diversity of products that even a medium-size winemaker brings to market in the United States?

The answer has its roots in climatic diversity. Within a few hundred miles of any winery in California can be found wide ranges of grape-growing conditions, each climatic zone supplying hospitable environment for several varieties of grapes. In the few hours a truck needs to cover the distance, the fresh grapes needn't suffer any deterioration. And, it takes a very modest vintner, indeed, to resist the temptation to broaden his product line.

Popular Myth

The versatility of the American vintner lays to rest one of the basic misconceptions of the wine business: that any small winery can make a better wine than a medium-sized one. Unquestionably, some of the small vintners are true artists. As long as they limit themselves to the few types of wine they make best, they may, with proper dedication, realize enormous satisfaction for themselves and their customers. They will not, of course, have enough products to fill the distributional pipeline to distant markets. Moreover, if one of them has growth ambitions, he might be tempted to compromise the quality of his product by filling orders with wines he buys from another producer, or he could sell his wines before they are fully matured. The small entrepreneur's biggest hurdle is that with his limited resources he can't hope to assemble the staff of cellarmaster, cooper, enologist, production manager, and all the others necessary for a smooth-flowing operation. His volume simply won't justify all that expense.

Akin to the sometimes unenlightened admiration for the "small winery" is the equally fallible dedication to "Chateau wines." Chateaus are romantically visualized as the bucolic retreats of the affluent French, growing prize grapes in limited quantity and crushing them for wines released only in limited quantities. There are, in fact, some idyllic, famous picture-book chateaus that grow and crush exquisite grapes and ferment them into wonderful, occasionally great wines. Invariably these wines are in scant supply, commanding prices that most of us would consider outrageous, but worth every penny, pfennig, yen, centime, or farthing to a wine collector who doesn't need to ask the price. There are, however, in the Bordeaux District of France many chateaus that fall short of the picture-book version. A château is not necessarily a castle. It can be a large operation or just a farm, a ranch, or a small vineyard producing a few thousand gallons, even a few thousand bottles, of wine per year. The owners normally have no sales organization or product recognition, and they sell their wines in the sixty-gallon barriques to a favored *négociant* in the city of Bordeaux. There is nothing necessarily dishonest or deceptive in this arrangement. The honorable *négociant* gives the wine loving care, perhaps filters off the last vestiges of lees, and bottles it under a label identifying the château of origin. Or, if he is a *négociant éleveur*, he may undertake through tender ministrations and aging to improve or upgrade the quality. In most cases, the "little Château" bottled by the *négociant* in Bordeaux is more reliable than that bottled at the non-classified château. Even some of the great chateaus allow wines of poor vintages to be bottled by *négociants*. Nevertheless, importers in the United States and England keep asking for the "château-bottled" wines.

Il est fils de boulanger il aime la baissure

Où l'hostesse est   belle le vin est bon

Belle hostesse
est un mal
pour la bource

Vin trouble ne
casse pas les dents

Les pierres
et les fem-
mes sont
toujours
en dangers et   Les armes d'Acteon

Vin du grand
tonneau
pendant quil est en
ça met à lessive
Et quil mesle de l'eau
parmi son vin claire
Le boulenger en haut
à sa femme lassitre
prennent d'aultres
plaisirs querux du cadran

Bottling on the Run

Frankly, one can no longer take without a pinch of salt the solemn declaration on the label, *Mise au château*, or *Mise en bouteille au château*, meaning "Bottled at the chateau" — the French equivalent of the American hallmark, "Estate-bottled." It must not be supposed that some of these "little château" wines are not, in

These contemporary linoleum cuts by Albert Volckerts feature wine bottles. The Christian Brothers Collection.

fact, bottled at the château; the amenities of strict adherence to the pledge of the label are met by a compact, mobile bottling plant on a truck bed that moves from château to château, enabling each of its vintner customers to label his wines, *Mise en bouteille au château.*

These apparently legal practices, other than tricking a gullible retail purchaser, do no great harm. In the long run, though, they tend to cast a shadow of doubt over all foreign wines a buyer hasn't tried before and to make him shy away if claims on the label seem extravagant. Besides, the product of the little château is usually so limited in volume that no continuity of supply can be expected, no matter whether bottled at the château or at the cellar in Bordeaux.

One final myth about rare wines needs to be dispelled — the one that puts the stamp of value on the bottle bearing the dust and cobwebs of time that's recovered after many years of aging from some dank cave or subterranean cellar. The fact is that caves and underground cellars harbor bacteria that are harmful to wine. From centuries back, they were pressed into service for wine storage because of their admirable uniformity of cool temperature, which is an ideal environment for a wine that is accumulating character and distinction with age. But the dangerous bacteria are invidious; they can even attack a wine through its moist cork. And, wines are so vulnerable that aging cellars are wisely separated from fermenting rooms; yeast cells in a new crush can be carried in the air and may start a refermentation in any aging wines containing vestigial grape sugar. Modern wineries, in Europe as well as in the United States, preserve an aging temperature between fifty-two and sixty degrees Fahrenheit by insulating their buildings and by air-conditioning that also sanitizes the atmosphere. The modern winery leaves little to chance.

6 Wine Goes to Market

*I*t is a phenomenon of American letters that more ink and unfettered hyperbole are dedicated to wine than to all other alcoholic beverages combined. Recent years have witnessed the birth of magazine after magazine devoted to the buying, storing, collecting, drinking, and serving of wine. Printing presses pour out a torrent of books, some of them from the pens of acknowledged authorities and many of them handsomely illustrated and bound. Daily newspapers and press syndicates have discovered an audience for wine writings, and the topic has achieved the crowning glory of recognition in a stream of weekly, biweekly, and monthly newsletters. All this is in addition to the foundation literature of the academic scientists and the long-established trade press.

A glance at The Christian Brothers collection of prized volumes in The Wine Museum will demonstrate that the phenomenon is neither purely American nor of recent origin. No matter how much we enjoy distilled spirits — and

the records indicate that some of us find a good deal of pleasure in them — it is hard to picture ourselves breathing a litany of ecstatic rhetoric over a highball of "Old Birdcage" and branch water. Yet, the wine literature of yesterday and today is flavored with a vocabulary, barely comprehensible to those outside a select circle, that approaches the incantations of a sybaritic ritual.

The Language of Wine

As an act of mercy to the uninitiated, it is suggested here that the experts' passion for the language of wine, however authoritative, may actually be a disservice to a person who is bewildered by such words as flinty, musty, corky, piquant, and precocious when used to describe subtle flavor characteristics of wine. To say that a wine is sweet is clear enough to all of us, and we learn easily that the opposite of sweet is not sour as in lemons and vinegar, but dry, lacking in sugar. But, if we say that a wine has finesse, or a good nose, or that it's hard or soft or velvety, we

express a nuance of taste that one learns only by experience. Roundness, body, bouquet, breeding — all these have a place in the argot of the sophisticate. To the novice, however, they could as easily be the mumbo jumbo of a jungle fertility rite for all the meaning they convey. And, what is more to the point here, they tend to discourage the uninitiated by giving the false notion that wine is the elixir of a chosen few.

All of which may be considered as the preamble to a new law, hereby promulgated, which will take its place in the annals of whimsical jurisprudence alongside Parkinson's Law, the Peter Principle, and Murphy's Law — the one that says that if anything can go wrong, it will. The new law will be known as The Wine Drinker's Law. Reduced to its essence, it will

Since ancient times, governments of most countries have taken some measure to regulate, and often tax, the making and sale of wines and other alcoholic beverages. Emperor Ferdinand III of Austria issued this ordinance regulating the retail sale of wine and beer on February 22, 1644. (Printed broadside).
The Christian Brothers Collection.

say that you don't have to take lessons, survive a blood test, or learn a new language to qualify as a member of the fraternity of wine drinkers.

The law ushers in a new era of permissiveness. It will be amply fortified with penalties. It will deprive of his corkscrew and tasting cup the purist who frowns when a citizen of The New Dispensation does one of the following:

— Demands of the waiter that his Burgundy be chilled.

— Washes down his rib roast with a Chablis or Sauterne instead of a Pinot Noir or Cabernet Sauvignon.

— Vacillates between Chianti and Zinfandel to complement his broiled swordfish.

The aim of the new law is not to discourage the purist in the exercise of his right to rhapsodize over wines, but rather to open the door and swing it wide in a gesture of welcome to the person who senses that he could enjoy wine if it were not encumbered with all that jargon of the connoisseur.

Self-Discovery

Underlying this new statute is a conviction that a person who finds pleasure in wine will, if left to his own devices, discover that coldness tends to dull the flavor of a red wine while enhancing that of a white or a Rosé; formulate his own standards of choosing a wine to complement a meal; and recognize that self-education is fun, even when you make mistakes. What this statute will expressly avoid is telling him "how" to drink wine. If he passes up the opportunity to find out for himself, he'll miss one of the sublime pleasures in wine — the joy of discovery.

The area open to exploration of wines is extensive. In Chapter III, we gave barely a hint of how extensive, in the notation that Californians — by reason of their proximity to the source of supply — have more or less immediate access to more than nine hundred brands and types of

During the late-nineteenth and early-twentieth centuries, California vintners hauled their barrels of wine on large horse-drawn wagons for delivery to the retailers. Photo courtesy Mirassou Vineyards.

varietal table wines made solely from California grapes. That estimate included none of the generic wines, sparkling wines, dessert wines, or modestly priced standard table wines, the kind you can buy in a jug for day-to-day use; nor did it include any foreign wines that flash their intriguing labels from retail shelves in California.

Actualités 581: — Cette année-ci le vin est du vin . . . dépèchez-vous d'en acheter . . . , je ne vous garantis pas qu'il restera toujours comme ça! . . . (Actualities 581: — This year the wine is really wine . . . hurry to buy some . . . , I cannot guarantee that it will always be the same . . .)

Honoré Daumier parodies a mid-nineteenth-century sales pitch in this lithograph from an 1858 issue of Charivari. The Christian Brothers Collection.

ACTUALITES .

— Cette année-ci le vin est du vin.......dépêchez-vous d'en acheter....,je ne vous garantis pas qu'il restera toujours comme ça !....

MAGASIN DE LA SOCIÉTÉ OENOPHILE.

Bottomless Cask

In the aggregate, American wines in their seemingly endless varieties are dwarfed numerically by the torrent of European wines that has gushed across the Atlantic in response to the great surge in wine consumption on this continent. Not all brands and types are available in any single store, but one analysis of the offerings up and down the East Coast indicated that more than ten thousand individual foreign and American wines were on sale. This adds a dimension of complexity to the searching consumer's choice of the one wine, or the dozen wines or the fifty wines that, in his lifetime, will appeal to him most. From such a multitude of choices, how does one even begin to make a selection?

Magasin de la Société Oenophile, *the warehouses of the Society of the Friends of Wine in Paris, is the subject of this lithograph from an 1838 issue of* Charivari. *Although wine was usually bought by the barrel, stored for further aging and then bottled when ready by the cellar staff, this huge wine cellar also housed thousands of bottles of aging fine wine for the society's members.* The Christian Brothers Collection.

It is the purpose of these lines to help cut a path through the thicket, not by saying that this is a good wine or that a bad one, but rather by identifying the procedures by which the individual will be encouraged to pronounce this judgment for himself.

A nineteenth-century French retail winestore, under the name "Caves Beaujolaises," offering wine by the glass at 10 centimes or by the liter at 40 c. for red and 50 c. for white, is the subject of this early-twentieth-century drypoint etching by Bror Julius Olsson Nordfeldt. The Christian Brothers Collection.

One indisputable truth is that you — Y-O-U — are not only the most competent but the only reliable judge of what you like and what you dislike. That goes for wine as much as it goes for apparel and for the dish from a restaurant menu. And, it's probably the central reason why vintners are encouraged to bring such a wide variety of products to the market.

You're going to need a supplier. In states where an agency of the Government is the sole supplier of wines and spirits, your search for a supplier ends almost as quickly as it begins. In the free-enterprise states, your choice probably lies between wine and liquor stores on the one hand and self-service supermarkets, discount stores, and possibly drugstores on the other.

par V. Adam

Carl: Vernet del.

V. Adam lith.

Marchand de Vins des environs de Rome

*A traveling wine merchant, his wagon laden with
wine barrels, is shown in the environs of Rome in this
nineteenth-century hand-colored lithograph by
Victor Adam (after a drawing by Carle Vernet).*
The Christian Brothers Collection.

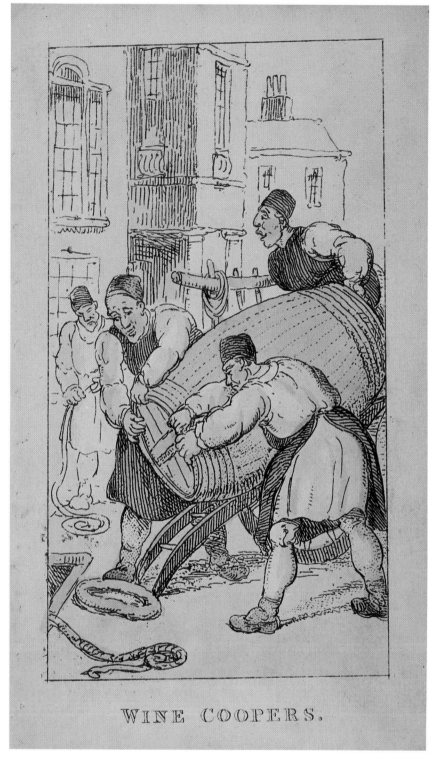

WINE COOPERS.

The Wine Coopers *are shown unloading a full cask of wine in this early-nineteenth-century hand-colored etching by Thomas Rowlandson from the* Cries of London *series. They wear the typical cooper's aprons.* The Christian Brothers Collection.

The Wine Party

Your primary object is to find a supplier who knows, drinks, and enjoys wines, and who knows how to display and store them. The informed wine merchant can save you time, trouble, and money by guiding you to wines that will meet your expressed needs and that are within your price range. It can be fun to experiment with unfamiliar wines, and anybody who enjoys wines will not resist the temptation to explore. Yet without a little guidance it can also be expensive and sometimes disappointing.

Foreign wines can be a challenge to most of us. You'll need the dealer's help in assessing their

In this hand-colored etching from Scenes from the Life of a Private Pupil, *published in 1850, the Englishman, George Cruikshank, turns his artist's eye on the Victorian middle class.* The Christian Brothers Collection.

probable worth and drinkability, for unless you're linguistically gifted, you could find the world of the foreign wine label a miasma of confusion. Many European wines, of course, are so well known and admired as to need no recommendation from the dealer. Moreover, the foreign

Above and opposite
Pre-Prohibition California retail wine stores offered
wine from the barrel and by the bottle for
off-premise consumption and by the glass for tasting
on the premises. Photo courtesy Mirassou Vineyards.

Note: The sign "We keep no books" meant
"No credit."

In this engraved broadside published by Nicolaes van Aelst in Rome during the first half of the seventeenth century, a list of all the wine that could be found in Rome is printed opposite a view of the interior of a Roman wine cellar with guests shown enjoying cheese and bread while sampling the different wines. The Christian Brothers Collection.

language on the label yields readily to the universal language of the senses when the bottle is opened. It's the lesser-known and the unknown wines that present a problem. The ultimate test, obviously, will come in the tasting. But, with your merchant's help, you can accomplish a preliminary screening by observing a few clues on the label — the name of the shipper and the name of the importer. You probably won't recognize either one, but if they're reliable a helpful dealer can show you other recognized products bearing their name and supporting their reputation.

Why, you may wonder, does one 1969 Médoc command a price a dollar higher than another produced the same year in the same part of the Bordeaux wine-growing region? Possibly the higher-priced one is really superior, or the importer has a better reputation. On the other hand, perhaps the importer of the less expensive wine was able to make an advantageous purchase by

Opposite
In this etching by Hermann Dyck, dated 1835, a German wine waiter is shown in the entrance to a wine cellar flanked by two large casks bearing the dates of good vintage years. He welcomes the visitor with a bottle and a glass of wine and wears a vintner's mallet in his belt for use in opening barrels at the bung or putting spigots into them. The Christian Brothers Collection.

Herbei, herbei zum vaterländischen Becher
Ihr Freunde, kommt herbei!
Preist diesen Trank als ächte deutsche Zecher
In froher Melodei!

Hermann Lycke 1835.

Engraved by R.H. Cromek Pupil of. Fran.ᶜ Bartolozzi RA.

The ROYAL CUMBERLAND

Tea Garden's and Tavern,

VAUXHALL.

placing an advance order, permitting him to shave his markup. The reliable wine merchant will know the answer and won't hesitate to explain it to you.

It's been noted that there are more than ten thousand distinctively different bottles of wine shown in the United States. No expert knows them all. No store can carry them all. Some brands improve the quality of their wines as they age, while others do not. The man behind the counter can advise you about them.

For the discriminating shopper in the wine store, there's a message in the price tag. It's well to remember that the era of the free lunch is past. In control states and in states with either price-posting regulations or fair-trade laws, bargain prices in wine are rare. That doesn't mean they're nonexistent. Like his fellow retailers, the wine merchant looks to impulse sales — that bottle of wine you hadn't intended to buy — to bolster his volume and his profit. Where it is permissible, he may try to stir that impulse with an especially attractive display or with a special offer that could, in fact, present you with an opportunity for a worthwhile purchase. Some people start their wine experience that way. But for some it is the first and last experience. It all depends on the wine and the merchant who put it on sale. If he has a transient clientele, he may not care. But if he wants to build repeat business among a growing number of appreciative customers, his price special may be a good buy. He may have made a special purchase of a good wine at an excellent price and perhaps wants to arouse your buying urge by sharing the saving with you.

Opposite
On a late-eighteenth-century engraved trade card for the Royal Cumberland Tea Gardens and Tavern, Vauxhall, the engraver Robert Hartley Cromek features a young Bacchus seated upon a barrel toasting the viewer with a glass of wine. The Christian Brothers Collection.

With that rare exception, though, the odds are that "specials" are not worth much more than is asked for them. The infallible test, if the bargain looks too good to pass up, is to buy a single bottle and taste it at home. If it's a dud, your loss is minimal. If it's truly an outstanding value, hustle back for more. Don't always expect the customary case-lot discount, though; some dealers disallow it on special-price deals.

There is, by the way, more than an attractive discount to justify case-lot buying, especially in foreign wines. With the great disparity between vintage years in foreign wines, your chances of buying another bottle of that delightful Bordeaux you enjoyed a few weeks ago are remote. If you find a wine that's pleasing, your cue is to go back for a case or two while it's still available.

For the thrifty consumer, comparison shopping for wine is as advisable as it is for any other commodities. And this applies not only to the less expensive everyday wines but to the fine wines as well. One useful procedure that saves steps is to ask several wine merchants to add your name to the mailing list to receive their periodic merchandise announcements. Often, you'll find that some of the special vintages of château-bottled Bordeaux wines are sold at different prices by different importers and different stores. In the fine wines, it's not only a matter of price but also of availability, for there are very limited supplies of them in the vast distributional labyrinth.

And, unless you have access to comparative wine tastings, which will be discussed later, it's only through comparison shopping and tasting that you'll discover the distinctions between two wines of identical type.

With practice, you'll also learn whether a wine merchant gives roughly comparable prominence to wines of roughly equal quality and stature. If you detect a wide gap, there may be room to suppose that he gives a heftier push to the products that return a better profit.

There are a few wine merchants who bring to their business an atmosphere approaching that of a boutique or atelier, where the patron and sales representative may sit in private discussion without the urgent ring of the cash register to disturb them; or where the attention given to meticulous care of inventory distinguishes the owner as one who respects wine.

There are also some who stock a modest number of wines so expensive — twenty-five to fifty dollars a bottle — that they're displayed under lock in a transparent case. That's not mere showmanship. The dealer expects to sell those wines and he can't afford to risk pilferage. If he has customers who can reach that price bracket, it's a safe bet that he has earned some service stripes as a wine merchant.

The other side of that coin is the undercapitalized retailer who stocks only a few bottles of many different types, varieties, and brands to create the illusion of a wide selection. If he isn't prepared to sell you a case after you've tried and enjoyed one bottle, you're certainly entitled to ask him why — and to evaluate his answer.

Narrowing the Choice

It's a formidable task to choose, from all the possibilities, the relatively small number of wines that appeal to individual taste. It's a little less so if you can find the wine merchant who can guide you through the maze. Yet another factor that eases the task is the reality, however melancholy to contemplate, that among the seven billion gallons of annual world production, there's an abundance of cheap wine and a shortage of the premium grades. With a little diligence, you'll be able to spot the cheapies that sail across the Atlantic masked under flamboyant labels. When you realize that it costs as much in freight

A whimsical drawing for the wall decoration of an entrance to a wine cellar is the subject of this late-sixteenth-century engraving by Bernhard Zan.
The Christian Brothers Collection.

Opposite
Der Stadt-Weinkeller *is the subject of these nineteenth-century steel engravings by Johann Poppel, after Julius Gottheil. A traditional feature in major German cities is the city-hall restaurant; located in the basement, it has a well-stocked wine cellar and features large, and sometimes very ornate, wine casks.* The Christian Brothers Collection.

DER STADT-WEINKELLER.

Ein Abend am Rhein.

and duty to ship a bottle of inferior wine as it costs to send a bottle of the finest Bordeaux or Moselle, the cheap wine loses much of its appeal.

All the foreign wines must conform to U.S. regulations requiring labels to specify in English the category of wine in the bottle, the alcoholic content, the quantity, and the name and address of the importer and the shipper. The rest is left to the conscience of the label designer, whose rhetoric and lithography have made this an art form. Regrettably, some practitioners haven't yet mastered the technique of bringing the contents up to the artistic level of the label. Much of the wine is disappointing.

Reading wine labels is almost a science in itself. Each country has its own label require-

A happy gathering of people are shown enjoying themselves at an outdoor restaurant above the Rhine River in this anonymous late-nineteenth-century lithograph after a painting by Christian Eduard Bottcher, entitled Ein Abend am Rhein. *The Christian Brothers Collection.*

ments. While the laws of the United States have been adopted to protect the consumer, the labeling laws of some European countries were more likely inspired by a desire to protect the producer. France, notably, adopted laws originally to shield the individual producer as well as one producer from another; only subsequently did the consumer get any consideration. The creation of the European Economic Community and its Common Market had as one of its attributes a long-range plan to unify wine regulations and laws, a process that's well along today in Germany.

Growth Classification

France, probably more than any other European country, has tried to relieve the chaos enshrouding the designation of its wines, at least its fine wines. The French, as far back as the middle of the nineteenth century, instituted a rigid arrangement of priorities among the wines of some four thousand vineyards in the Bordeaux region. This was the so-called 1855 classification of growths, a process by which a panel of judges selected the clarets of sixty-one identified chateaus in the Médoc District and the white wines of twenty-five chateaus in the Sauternes District, grouping them in order of the quality they then possessed. Three or four generations later, the original classifications still stamp their cachet on the wines of the designated chateaus. Some new classifications are now in the offing. In the United States, where the growing of fine wines has had only four decades to establish a tradition, it's worth pondering that a name like Château Lafite-Rothschild, or Château Margaux, or Château d'Yquem commands the same worldwide veneration today that it received well over a century ago.

By the same process, in 1953 thirteen red and eight white wines of the Graves District were chosen and classified, and in 1955 official classifications were conferred on seventy-five top clarets of Saint-Émilion. If your budget permits subjective exploration of the French wine classifications, your dealer may be able to show you the entire mouth-watering list of the chosen; or you can find it in any of the excellent wine books and encyclopedias available for sale and in the public library. It will help your perspective, though, to bear in mind that the classifications apply only to the wines of the Bordeaux region, not to those of Burgundy's Côte d'Or, the neighboring Mâcon and Beaujolais areas, or to the Chablis District nearby. Nor do they include the wines of Alsace, the Côtes du Rhône, the Loire Valley, the Mediterranean areas of Midi and Côte de Provence, the northern slopes of the Pyrenees, and the Côtes du Jura on the Swiss border. Excluded from the classifications also are France's celebrated champagnes and brandies, which constitute virtually independent principalities within the French wine realm.

Controls Applied

To fortify her reputation as the cradle of great wines, France has taken stern measures to prevent exploitation of the better ones. Control is exercised through a law referred to as *Appellation d'Origine Contrôlée*. The law applies to only about 20 percent of the total French vineyard acreage. It defines the geographic boundaries of the principal wine-producing regions and specific areas, including the Champagne regions of Reims and Épernay northeast of Paris and the brandy zones of Cognac and Armagnac in the vicinity of Bordeaux. It limits the volume of fine-wine production by each vineyard through a system of local control boards reporting to a master control in the capital. Wines authorized under this system bear on the label the words, *Appellation Contrôlée*.

In addition, the labels declare in what circumstances the wine reaches the market. The fine wines of Bordeaux carry one of four legends: the familiar *Mise en bouteille au château*, meaning that the wine was fermented, aged, finished, and bottled at the château named on the label from the vineyard's own grapes; *Mise en bouteille par (name of merchant)*, for wines sold in the cask by chateaus and bottled and marketed by a wine merchant; *Monopole*, or "private brand," for wines blended and bottled and distributed by the merchant; or the name of the parish or district (such as *Graves, Pomerol*, or just plain Bordeaux), which indicates that the contents is a blend of wines from the district on the label, and that it is bottled and marketed by a merchant. Some quality Burgundy wines are labeled *Mise en bouteilles à la propriété* or *Mise au domaine*, also meaning "Estate-bottled," the end product of an integrated operation from grape cultivation and harvest through crushing, fermenting, aging, packaging, and distribution. Because Burgundy's vineyards are small, the vast bulk of its wines are bottled and distributed by the wine merchant, whose good name becomes an important assurance of quality.

Types Parisiens. I: Eh bien malin! comment le trouvez vous celui-la! — Oui, oui . . . mais enfin — oui . . . oui . . . oui! (Parisian Characters. I: *"Very well, you sharpie, how do you like this one! — Yes, yes . . . but then — yes . . . yes . . . yes!"*) *One of the many lithographs relating to wine by Honoré Daumier from* Charivari. The Christian Brothers Collection.

TYPES PARISIENS.

Eh bien malin! comment le trouvez vous celui-la! — Oui, oui . . . mais enfin — Oui . . . oui . . . oui!

Italy, and to some degree Spain and Germany, have also been moving in this direction of providing solid information on the label. In this respect, the Old World of Europe is following the lead of the New World. Post-Prohibition laws of the United States are more restrictive than those of Europe, and some states have added their own twists, usually for tax purposes but often for protecting indigenous industry against encroachment from other states. One important thrust of California law as it affects wine is to establish quality standards that cannot be circumvented by label rhetoric.

When Germany overhauled its wine law in 1971, it established three product classifications that serve as a guide to the consumer:

Deutscher Tafelwein (German table wine), sometimes called *Konsumwein*. These are light, simple, but pleasant wines from defined areas and made from approved grape varieties. The label identifies the region or township but not the vineyard of origin.

Qualitätswein bestimmter Anbaugebiete (quality wine of designated regions) is wine of above-average quality produced in clearly defined areas from approved grape varieties. It must pass Government analysis and taste test and always carry a control number on the label, which may also identify village and vineyard.

Qualitätswein mit Prädikat (quality wine with special attributes) is the highest classification, granted for such attributes as *Kabinett* (made from fully matured grapes grown in a specific district); *Spätlese* (superior wine from grapes picked after normal harvest); *Beerenauslese* (made from individually selected, very ripe grapes); *Auslese* (from selected grapes); and *Trockenbeerenauslese* (from grapes that were picked when dried on the vine and very sweet).

Labels on these quality wines of designated regions and with special attributes may name the vineyard of origin, the village or district, the region, vintage year, grape variety, name of bottler, name of producer, and trade name or trademark. If the wine is estate-bottled, the label may read *Erzeugerabfüllung* (bottled by the producer) and *Aus eigenem Lesegut* (from his own grapes).

All eleven official grape-growing areas are in the western part of Germany along the Rhine, the Moselle, and their tributaries.

Although Italy is the largest wine producer in the world, many of its wines never reach the export market. This is not only because Italians are big consumers as well as producers, but also because some of the country's more desirable wines are too delicate to stand the rigors of travel. The Government has since 1963 supervised production. It issues special certificates of origin for many types of wine from the major vineyard areas such as Piedmont, Lombardy, Veneto, Tuscany, Umbria, Latium, and Campania. The legend on the label that reads *Denominazione di Origine Controllata* verifies the controlled origin of the wine and the compliance of its producer with quality regulations.

Below the Pyrenees
Spain and Portugal produce large quantities of table wines for both domestic consumption and export, particularly Rosé wines in recent years. The two countries south of the Pyrenees have been more noted for their fortified wines, Spain for its sherries and Portugal for its port. They, like Portugal's offshore island of Madeira that produces the distinctive dessert wine of the same name, enjoy far warmer climate than France and hence sweeter grapes. This natural sweetness is retained by adding grape brandy to the must that arrests fermentation by halting the conversion of sugar into alcohol and carbon dioxide. Because of the "fortification" with brandy, these dessert wines reach the market with an alcohol content between 17 and 20 percent, compared with about 12 percent for table wines. They differ also in that they usually need longer aging in the cask to reach full maturity.

U.S. Imports Grow
More and more American wines are exported every year, and on the home front they've

taken long strides in increasing consumer acceptance. It was noted earlier that Americans more than doubled their use of wine in a fifteen-year span, and that the big surge in popularity was in table wines. Imports also rose in acceptance, and they now have between 15 and 20 percent of the U.S. market. American wines serve the other 80 percent.

Upstate New York (notably the Finger Lakes region), Ohio, New Jersey, Michigan, Missouri, and a number of other states supplied about 10 percent of the nation's needs in 1978.

California vineyards, then, account for about 70 percent of the wine that Americans drink; and Californians, as if in a salute to home industry, manage to drink almost a quarter of the total. In harmony with its dominant position, the state has adopted the strongest laws governing standards of wine quality and purity, winery sanitation and labeling. The long, hot Central Valley that stretches almost three hundred miles from the state capital in Sacramento to the foothills of the Tehachapi Mountains south of Bakersfield is far and away the major producing area. In its abundant summer heat, the grapes that can adapt to that climate mature quickly, and year in and year out they account for 99 percent of the state's dessert wines and better than 80 percent of its table wines. Coastal vineyards extending north from Monterey through San Francisco and almost to the Oregon border produce somewhat less than 20 percent of California's table wines, but they are primarily still and sparkling wines of distinctive flavor and aroma from low-yielding vines whose grapes mature slowly under the influence of warm summer days and cool evening breezes from the Pacific. In the coastal belt, the principal producing areas are the famous Napa Valley and the counties of Sonoma, Mendocino, Alameda, Santa Clara, San Benito, Monterey, and Santa Cruz.

The Stiffest Controls

Elsewhere in this volume we have referred to the United States' and California's stern statutory controls. It may be useful to group the main ones here:

Sugar: California is stiff-necked about added sweetening. It insists that all sugar and alcohol in California still wines be derived from grapes. California vintners can well live with that regulation, certainly more comfortably than their contemporaries in the East and in Europe because their grapes get enough sun to develop their optimum natural sweetness.

In addition to this restriction, the following Federal controls prevail:

Estate-bottled: The words may be used on the label only if the vintner claiming responsibility for the contents has fermented all the wine from grapes grown in the proximity of his winery and under his supervision. Since no winery of even moderate size can grow all the grapes it needs, not many wines may be so classified.

Vintage date: On a label it means that at least 95 percent of the grapes in that wine were grown and crushed that year. (Most European countries stipulate a minimum of only 75 percent.) Some wine drinkers, beguiled by the mystique of the vintage year associated with European wines, mistakenly think of the date as an enduring guarantee of quality. It is not.

Geographical origin: A declaration of origin is required on the label. If the label says "New York State," then at least 75 percent of the grapes must have been grown in New York. (However, California law requires that when a wine is labelled "California," that 100 percent of the grapes come from within its borders.) If the wine is described as Napa Valley wine, at least 75 percent of the grapes must have been grown in that area.

Varietal labeling: To qualify as a varietal wine bearing the name of a specific grape variety such as Pinot Saint George, or Cabernet Sauvignon, at least the legal minimum of the wine must be from that grape and it must get its predominant taste, aroma, and characteristics from that grape.

Produced and bottled by: In this case, it is the bottler who was responsible for crushing,

aging, and finishing at least 75 percent of the wine.

Made and bottled by: Here the bottler made at least 10 percent of the wine by crushing, aging, and finishing.

Cellared and bottled by, Prepared and bottled by, and *Perfected and bottled by:* These labels indicate to the buyer that the bottler performed some finishing procedure.

Bottled by: The minimum legal requirement on the label, it means exactly what it says and no more. The phrase must be followed by the bottler's name and place of business.

In this late-nineteenth-century etching by Ernest Forberg (after a painting by Eduard Kurzbauer) two gentlemen are eagerly anticipating a comment from the third who is tasting two different wines — one poured from the carafe on the table and the other from the wine thief held by the cellarmaster. (The wine thief is used for drawing samples from the wine barrels through the bunghole.) The Christian Brothers Collection.

Alcoholic strength: The percentage must be declared. Table wines are allowed to range up to 14 percent alcohol, dessert and appetizer wines 17 to 21 percent.

In a plate from the early-nineteenth-century series Musée Grotesque *by G. de Cari, the vintner asks,* "Comment le trouvez-vous?" *(How do you like this wine?).* The Christian Brothers Collection.

World Scene

A good four-fifths of present worldwide production is in Europe, with Italy out in front and France second. They are followed in order by Spain, USSR, Argentina, United States, Portugal, and Germany. The *Office International de la Vigne et du Vin* lists forty-four wine-growing countries on all five continents. Some additional countries that export wines to the United States are Austria, Australia, Bulgaria, Chile, China, Greece, Hungary, Israel, Switzerland, Yugoslavia, and Russia.

Movement of wine into the marketplace has undergone as much change in the years since Prohibition as has the public's taste and capacity for it. Where not too long ago the American consumer overwhelmingly preferred the rich, fortified dessert wines such as sherry and port, he has now shown preference for light table wines and, in the case of younger people, also for the flavored "pop" or "mod" wines. And, where in years past the consumer in New Jersey may have chosen a bottle of California wine that traveled cross-country in tankcar, or even tankship, to be bottled in the East, the chances are that the same vintner's wines are now bottled at the winery and shipped as case goods in so-called jumbo rail cars. In fact, the two largest single producers of California wines, the E. & J. Gallo Winery in Modesto and the United Vintners, Inc., in San Francisco, even make all or part of their own glass bottles.*

In the first quarter-century or so following Repeal, much California wine was shipped in bulk to local bottlers in all parts of the United States, who then packaged it under their own labels, carrying no identification of the actual producer. Subsequently, as competitive promotion and consumer sophistication made buyers more brand conscious, this type of merchandising declined. Today, most California wineries package their own products and sell them through distributors strategically located in the principal consumption centers.

* Californians have no monopoly on the bottle plant integrated into the wine-production system. Overseas publications tell of at least one large French bottler of *vins ordinaire* and *vins du pays* who has a plastic blow-molding machine insinuated into the production line. It forms a plastic container and a few seconds later the container flashes past the spout of the filling machine, then on to the capping unit. For wines that are intended to be drunk when fresh, this system may be both efficient and adequate.

Bottling and all the processes leading up to it are meshed toward a single objective, providing a product that's irresistible to the consumer. The finest as well as the poorest wines are made to be sold and drunk, and above all appreciated, because the winegrower wants you to come back for more. The only way to find out if the wine is irresistible is to taste it.

Winery Tours

Those of us fortunate enough to live in or near a winegrowing area have one inexpensive, pleasurable way to satisfy our curiosity — a winery tour. In upstate New York, in California, and in other states, wineries usually are eager to have visitors. The visit, at regularly scheduled hours, not only gives the vintner an audience interested in what he has to say about his wines but also provides him with useful feedback as the visitors taste and react vocally. The *quid pro quo* for the visitor is that he has the opportunity to taste perhaps half a dozen wines without the expense of buying them; if he finds one he likes, he is usually able to buy it on the spot and may later continue to buy it at his local merchant. In an area like the Napa Valley of California, virtually the only limit on the extent of the tour is the visitor's time, capacity, and staying power, for there's a succession of excellent wineries with hospitable tasting rooms.

Travel agents, local chambers of commerce, or civic officials in the United States and their equivalent in Europe's most popular wine regions— Bordeaux, Burgundy, and the valleys of the Rhine and the Moselle, for example—supply visitors with information about wine tours. In California, the Wine Institute (165 Post Street, San Francisco, California 94108) has it all wrapped up in an attractive free booklet.

Tasting Party

There's a drawback, of course, to the winery tour — the lack of opportunity to compare the wines of a single type produced by several vintners. Unless you have a true wine taster's memory, you won't remember how one winery's Cabernet Sauvignon tasted when you get

WINE	APPEARANCE (color; clarity)	AROMA (bouquet)	TASTE (body)	TOTALS

Grade each of the three characteristics on a scale of 1 to 10.

to the second and the third tasting rooms. Group wine tastings circumvent that problem. Often a social organization — a club, a lodge, or a church society — stages a fund-raising wine tasting that offers for comparison the wines of several wineries. Here, direct comparisons are possible, and if you're able to articulate your taste perceptions or even grade them, say, on a scale of one to ten, you'll want to keep notes on them. Sometimes, at a tasting of this sort the sponsor will provide you with a program listing all the wines, with space for your comments.

The "score card" is more common at tastings held periodically by such semiprofessional organizations as the Wine & Food Society, the Gourmet Society, the Medical Friends of Wine,

the Lawyer Friends of Wine, the Military Order of Wine Tasters, and Les Amis du Vin. If such a group exists in your area, you may qualify for membership or possibly know a convivial friend who belongs and will invite you to be his guest at a tasting.

There are, of course, the official wine tastings by panels of impartial, qualified experts who judge the products of competing vintners on an impartial basis and reward the winners with medals of gold, silver, and bronze. These medals are meaningful to you if they are clearly part of an award-winning pattern that stamps the vintner as a consistent winner. It shows that he is straining for high quality and often succeeding.

Finally, you can always organize your own

tasting session. It need be neither expensive nor extensive. Instead of cocktails before dinner, serve your guests a small selection of wines in modest tasting-quantities. The form at left can be adapted to your needs so that guests may keep a record of what they've tasted and perhaps even compete for a prize in a blind tasting.

Make up your own rules and procedures. For a group of six, half-bottles of six wines will do. Starting with the most delicate white wines and progressing through the most full-bodied reds, serve each person about two ounces from each bottle successively, allowing them time to jot down their impressions before bringing on the next bottle. If it's a "blind" competition, be sure the label is concealed. You can, if you wish, challenge your guests with such questions as: Is it American or European? If American, is it from California, New York, Ohio? If European, is it French, German, Italian? If French, is it from Bordeaux, Burgundy, Loire, Rhône? If German, is it a Moselle or a Rhine? Can they even name the type?

For a simple comparison tasting, they can grade each of the specified characteristics on a scale of one to ten, the totals determining which of the six wines is the evening's favorite.

A "triangle tasting" can enliven proceedings. Choose two wines of the same type — use two bottles of one vintner, one bottle of another brand — making certain that the bottles are identically shaped but well masked. Then invite your guests to taste them all and determine which two samples represent the same wine.

Tasting, you will agree, is what it's all about.

During the nineteenth century and earlier, large containers, such as these of copper, brass, and pewter from Austria and Germany, would be used to carry wine from the cellar to the upper floors for serving. (left to right: 13" high, 15¼" high, 11" high.)
The Christian Brothers Collection.

7 Wine is for Drinking

Anyone who has examined the Franz W. Sichel collection of glass drinking-vessels in The Wine Museum of San Francisco — or even the pictures of specimens from it that illustrate this book — can understand why, in centuries past, there existed an element of snobbery in the ceremony of wine drinking. Many of the glasses that the German-born vintner and his family accumulated in their travels are elegant beyond belief, prize examples of the art of glass blowing, cutting, engraving, and enameling from the ateliers of renowned artists in Venice, Bavaria, Bohemia, Belgium, England, and Holland. Drinking mere water from such glasses would lift the soul. How much more enjoyable, then, would be the drinking of the wines of the day, even though these were — by the standards we now enjoy — quite primitive.

There's a message in the Sichel collection for those of us who enjoy wine, or may in the future be intrigued by the mystique of it. What it says is that wine makes its appeal not alone to our senses of taste and smell; it offers us visual delight as well. The earliest vintners discovered that, and when they went on to discover how much the artistry of the glassmaker enhanced their wines, their pride in both was boundless.

You can prove it to yourself with a little experiment. Choose a wine you enjoy, pour a little into a jelly glass and a little into the clearest, thinnest glass you own, then take a sip from each. Your senses of taste, smell — and sight — will tell you more about the serving of wine than all the books written on the subject can ever impart.

The chances are that the play of the light on the wine in the finer glass, the "tears" and "legs" that festoon the inner wall when you swirl the wine, and the flattering enhancement of color imparted by the clear glass will add visual appeal to the taste of the wine and to the aroma that rises from it.

There is no "proper" way to serve wine, just as there is no "proper" way to select a wine for a given purpose. In both cases, individual taste

In northern Europe, tankards were used not only for drinking but also for serving; the large mid-sixteenth-century oak and pewter daubenkrug *from Saxony (center) was probably made as a container for bringing the wine up from the cellar. 11½" high. The Christian Brothers Collection.*

is the criterion that prevails. Rather than blindly accept the dicta of the self-proclaimed experts regarding which shape glass with which wine, it can be fun to blaze your own trails in the selection of your wineglasses.

It's no accident that wineglasses seem to come in all shapes and sizes, even colors. The bewildering variety is the result of the manufacturers' differing concepts of what a wineglass should be and what it should look like. There are no "official" sizes, capacities, shapes, or colors. Your own reason will tell you, when you reflect on the matter, that a dainty two-ounce glass is no more adequate for the wine you drink with your dinner than for the water, tea, coffee, or milk you serve at the meal; nor would you be likely to choose an eighteen-ounce dinner wineglass for a sip of sherry.

The All-Purpose Glass

Still, it is no overstatement to say that a single glass can serve all your wine needs and do it tastefully. Some years ago, California's Wine Institute came up with what its designers called an all-purpose wineglass. Made of clear, colorless glass, it's tulip-shaped and rises from a stem one and three-quarters inches high. The overall height of the glass is five and a half inches; its brim capacity, eight ounces.

Others, too, have produced all-purpose glasses of different design, height, and capacity. Two qualities most of them share are aesthetic appeal and comparatively low cost. No matter how one may later supplement his collection, some all-purpose glasses will always be desirable for

After many years of aging, some wines develop sediment, and in order to eliminate this residue at the time of serving, the bottles of wine are placed in cradles or carefully poured into decanters, sometimes with the aid of special funnels. The Christian Brothers Collection.

serving table wines. The stem lifts the bowl high enough to accentuate the color of the wines and to distinguish the blush of the Rosé from the red of the Burgundy and the various hues of the white wines. And, holding the glass by the stem instead of the bowl prevents transfer of body heat from the hand to the wine, an important consideration when the wine is chilled. (Grasping the foot of the glass between thumb and forefinger, a custom among some vintners and aficionados, can be tricky; hold onto the stem unless you're prepared for the consequences of anointing the dinner cloth.)

Ideal Portion

Three to four ounces of wine in the seven- or eight-ounce all-purpose glass are an ideal portion. Less would seem skimpy, while more would rob you of the aroma that is captured in the upper bowl as it rises from the gently

A collection of late-eighteenth- and nineteenth-century English and French decorative wine labels such as these are an outgrowth of the need to identify decanters and bottles filled with wine from the cellar. Mr. and Mrs. Alfred Fromm Collection.

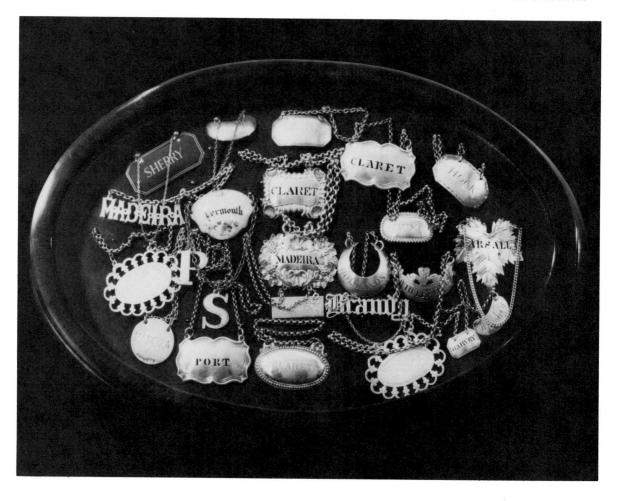

Brother Timothy, F.S.C., Cellarmaster of The
Christian Brothers Winery in the Napa Valley,
shown with his prized corkscrew collection.

Among the many niceties of elegant wine service are the decorative corks that artists have created for use at the table after the original bottle cork has been extracted, such as these English Derby painted porcelain-topped corks from the early nineteenth century. The Christian Brothers Collection.

swirled wine. You have deliberately chosen, in other words, an oversize glass to permit you to enjoy the bouquet. And, it should be clear now why restaurants that serve wine in glasses scarcely larger than thimbles don't attract wine-buying patrons.

To say that the all-purpose glass is a suitable one for champagnes and other sparkling wines is to sow the seeds of controversy—or rather to nourish the seeds already sown. Ever since the legendary Dom Pérignon felt the first tickle of the "stars" on his palate three centuries ago, men have groped for the ideal drinking vessel. They searched for one that would both enhance the dazzle of the bubbles rising from no visible source, but also attenuate their release, thereby preserving the ceremonial glitter for a longer period.

The Better Champagne Glass

Who knows how many have quietly cursed the saucer-on-a-stem champagne glass when a gentle nudge on the elbow sent the wine cascading over the brim? In the hollow-stemmed variety, the saucer glass was partially redeemed by the columns of bubbles rising in the stem, but the visual spectacle was offset by the difficulty of washing the glass. Certainly more practical is the nine-ounce tulip champagne glass, more slender than the all-purpose and therefore a more spectacular stage setting for the display of bubbles. More slender still is the so-called flute glass, a tall wisp of crystal slightly reminiscent of a Pilsner beer glass except that it's much more delicate and graceful. Popular in Europe for more than a century, the flute glass is now winning a widening acceptance in the United States.

If Champagne is a couple-of-times-a-year event in your home, buying special glasses could be a luxury because the all-purpose glass would fill the need. But if you enjoy Champagne enough to serve it more often, your best bet is probably the flute glass.

For sherries and ports, the all-purpose glass is on the generous side. But there's no reason why you have to serve more in that seven-ounce glass than in a more conventional sherry glass of

Jacob Verzelini, born in Venice in 1522, emigrated to England in 1571. In 1575 he received a patent from Queen Elizabeth and the sole privilege (for twenty-one years) of producing glasses in the Venetian manner for the English market. The goblet here pictured is from his workshop and was first described in an 1770 inventory of the Duchess of Northumberland as "a very ancient glass, said to be Queen Elizabeth's, made in 1590." In addition to the arms of the Vintner's Company enclosed by a scrolling border and a shield between two vine branches each bearing a bunch of grapes, the design upon the glass includes abstracts from the arms of London, various legends, and the date 1590. 7¼" high. Franz Sichel Glass Collection.

An interesting drinking cup commemorating the Tailors Guild of Nuremberg, Germany. In the shape of a large thimble, this gold- and silver-plated copper cup is dated 1586 and bears the names of the guild members. 5½" high. Mr. and Mrs. Alfred Fromm Collection.

three to four and a half ounces. Indeed, the normal three-ounce serving of sherry in the eight-ounce glass will yield its bouquet with a fine flourish. The same can be said of brandy, which appeals almost equally to the senses of taste and smell; the all-purpose glass, though less bulbous than a conventional brandy snifter, provides plenty of swirling room for the normal one and a half ounce serving, and the bowl rests comfortably in the palm for the gentle warming that releases the exotic vapors for sniffing.

Once you have satisfied yourself that the all-

purpose wine glass is indeed a glass for all wines and that you may use it as such without fear of being stigmatized by social arbiters, your interest could turn to some of the special-purpose glasses. Like the all-purpose glass, they are available in a wide range of prices to suit just about any budget.

Clear Glass Preferred

One word of caution: You'll be sacrificing visual aesthetics if you choose a colored or tinted glass. There was a time when wines were cloudy or drab, and it was an act of mercy to serve them in a gaily decorated vessel discreetly tinted to mask the imperfections. That day is past. It's true that some European wines still may throw off a little sediment or precipitate a film of tannin, but careful decanting or serving will overcome that. American enologists have learned to make clean, sediment-free wines without excessive filtration that might rob them of their distinctive flavor accents.

Clear glass, then, is your best choice if you want to enjoy the visual treat of light playing on the wine as on a prism. As a general principle, the thinner the glass, the more it appeals to one's senses of touch and sight. And, take a tip from that resourceful man behind the bar: before serving, polish that glass until it glistens; the sparkle adds an extra dimension of enjoyment to the wine that the vintner was so careful to deliver at the peak of its brilliance.

Professional wine tasters are even more fastidious. They insist that their glasses be rinsed with clear warm water and hung, inverted, to drip-dry. Soaps and detergents often leave an unpleasant or at least unwanted odor that can spoil the flavor and aroma of wine. Tasters draw the line at dishtowels, even a fresh one.

Four- to four-and-a-half-ounce sherry glasses, to be served partly full, would probably be the most useful point of departure from exclusive use of all-purpose glasses. The same glass will also be appropriate for the three-ounce portion of port wine or Madeira that's customarily served, and if the body is bowl shaped with a constricted lip to imprison the aroma, it can

This German Reichsadlerhumpen *of smokey-colored glass was made in honor of the Holy Roman Emperor. It bears the double-headed eagle of the empire with the names and arms of the member states on its wings and is dated 1590. 12" high. Franz Sichel Glass Collection.*

Roemers are a specific type of drinking glass that developed in the Rhine country of Germany and the Netherlands. This late-seventeenth-century example from the Low Countries has a globular bowl opening into a hollow stem that bears three raspberry prunts and a foot containing a high kick. 7⅛" high. Franz Sichel Glass Collection.

also serve ideally as a brandy snifter. A person with a penchant for brandy probably won't be happy, though, with any substitute for a snifter from the tiny three-ounce bowl — which really isn't adequate for a serving of brandy — through the six-and-a-half-ounce size that's both ceremonial and inexpensive, to the large, showy bubble of gossamer crystal holding fourteen, eighteen, or even twenty ounces but still cud-

This seventeenth-century façon de Venise *wineglass with dark blue and clear waffle-pinched circular additions is typical of the applied decoration originating in Venice in the sixteenth century. 5" high.* Franz Sichel Glass Collection.

An early-eighteenth-century façon de Venise *wineglass has a hollow tapered stem with applied light-blue scroll and colorless crosshatched circular attachments. 4½" high.* Franz Sichel Glass Collection.

dling only two ounces of brandy. If you operate on a Cognac-style budget, or have discovered the recent advance that has been made by The Christian Brothers in their XO Rare Reserve brandy, this showpiece of the glassmaker's art won't be out of place in your collection.

Switching from all-purpose to wine goblet for red dinner wines, to the tall-stemmed hock glasses for whites, to single-purpose champagnes, to apéritifs — these are choices you'll no doubt make as and when the spirit moves you, or perhaps not at all. When you learn how a piece of flawless lead crystal can add to your enjoyment of a favored wine, your only problem may be a budgetary one.

Glass-Blowing Art

In this respect we may count ourselves lucky. Until a few years ago, the stemmed wineglass of graceful contour could only be made by hand. Glass blowing gradually became an art and added elegance to the primitive drinking vessels that had been the standard since Biblical times. The exquisite designs turned out by hand craftsmen since the fifteenth century account for many of the choice specimens in the Franz W. Sichel collection. But the machine age rolled past the glass blower until relatively recent years, when it became possible to produce some excellent glasses by machine and, in the mass-production process, drastically reduce prices. They are still somewhat heavier than the hand-crafted glass, and when flicked with a fingernail or spoon don't respond with the same bell-like tone that peals forth from a glass of pure crystal.

Now that the machine age has overtaken the drinking-glass industry, American manufacturers of "everyday" glassware are producing some very appealing glasses that are available in such price-oriented outlets as variety stores. German, Swiss, French, Czechoslovakian, and Mexican glass manufacturers have also been exporting some attractive but inexpensive products to the United States. Hardware, discount, and department stores, as well as those massive outlets for imported wares that are the American equiva-

The arched panels in two registers of this colorfully enameled humpen *depict the traditional "Ten Ages of Man." The piece was made in Bohemia during* the late-sixteenth or early-seventeenth-century. *11⅛" high.* Franz Sichel Glass Collection.

Interior of an Inn on a Hillside near Rome, *hand-colored etching, dated 1820, by Bartholomeo Pinelli.* The Christian Brothers Collection.

The Good Wine Tasters, *nineteenth-century hand-colored lithograph by Claude Thielley (after Johann Peter Hasenclever).* The Christian Brothers Collection.

lent of the Persian bazaar, offer wine glasses of good design in the all-purpose or goblet size for less than a dollar.

You can scale all the way up to as much as twenty-five or thirty dollars for a single glass made by American and European manufacturers of exquisite crystal. It's debatable, when you ponder some of the stratospheric prices, whether a thirty-dollar glass can improve your wine that much. Fortunately, that's a problem most of us don't have to deal with, for between one dollar and thirty dollars there's a price for just about every budget.

The Elegant Dinner

A carefully and laboriously prepared dinner deserves the harmonious accompaniment of fine wine, often of a different wine with each course for perfect compatibility. The elegant way, then, is to serve each wine in a different glass. In the festive table setting, these glasses are usually arranged from right to left, horizontally or diagonally. The order in which the host serves his wines, determined by the sequence of food, is generally from the lighter to the heavier to the sweet; if wineglasses of different shapes are available, they are placed in the sequence in which the wines are poured. If water tumblers are included in the table setting, they are usually placed to the left of the wineglasses.

It may be worth noting that while food platters are offered to seated guests from their left, the wines are poured from the right. This convention arose from the fact that most people are right-handed, including the person serving the wine.

An early-eighteenth-century covered pokal, Russian or possibly German, bears the portrait bust of Peter the Great within the framed legend: Vivat Peter Alexander Magnus Szar Mos. *15¼" high with cover. Franz Sichel Glass Collection.*

This tall wineglass of mid-eighteenth-century English or possibly the Netherlands manufacture bears the Dutch engraved arms of the City of Leyden supported by two heraldic lions. 7⅝" high. Franz Sichel Glass Collection.

Representative of glasses commemorating friendship, this mid-eighteenth-century English glass engraved in the Netherlands bears two clasped hands issuing from clouds under a blazing sun and the legend, De Vriendschap. 7¾" high. Franz Sichel Glass Collection.

A late-eighteenth-century English wineglass with stipple engraving in the manner of David Wolff, depicting three cupids seated on clouds; one offers a glass of wine. 6⅞" high. Franz Sichel Glass Collection.

A useful adjunct to a collection of wine-glasses is a decanter, or carafe. Occasionally, if you decide to try foreign wines, you'll encounter one that has thrown off some sediment. By pouring it carefully into the decanter, you can make sure that the sediment stays in the bottle. With clean wines, though, the bottle is the ideal serving vessel, and besides, the label is there for all to see; indeed, even when you decant the wine to separate it from sediment, guests may enjoy seeing the bottle as well as the carafe on the table, for the label carries its pedigree.

You'll get more frequent use from the decanter for serving everyday wines, the wines you buy in an economy-sized container that would be awkward to handle at the dinner table.

Decanters, like glasses, come in all shapes, sizes, and prices. Restaurants that devote a little thought to wine service have carafes for their "house wines" in a range of sizes from the individual serving of perhaps seven or eight ounces, through the half-liter serving for two, which offers a shade more than a pint, to the full liter for four, just over a quart.

Decanters of tasteful design have the advantage of being decorative as well as useful, which probably accounts for the fact that they have become popular as gifts. In fine crystal they can be extremely expensive, but American manufacturers have stepped into the scene and offer well-designed carafes for a very reasonable price.

Pouring Technique

Another wine-service item that's both useful and distinctive is the wine coaster, a deep tray slightly larger in diameter than a bottle and usually of silver or silver plate, that almost literally pays for itself in preventing bottle stains on the dinner cloth.

There is a technique to pouring from a bottle that minimizes the risk of dripping: a simple twist of from one-eighth to one-quarter turn of the bottle as the pouring is being finished. If it is done quickly while the bottle is still in pouring position, it tends to distribute any lin-

This late-eighteenth-century fluted tumbler has a gilt rim and a scene of a woman and a dog by a fountain, also in gilt. 3⅛″ high. Franz Sichel Glass Collection.

European glass painters drew upon many subjects to enhance their glasses — here on a late-nineteenth-century German goblet a figure of a violinist is shown accompanied by two cupids. 7½″ high. Franz Sichel Glass Collection.

gering drip around the mouth of the bottle. It's no guarantee, though, that after two or three glasses of wine have been poured, some won't run down the side of the bottle when it is returned to its place. If its place is a coaster, the bottle will leave its ring in the coaster, where it will do no harm, and not on the tablecloth. If you don't have a wine coaster and prefer not to

Opposite
A late-nineteenth-century German drinking horn with engraved gilt-brass ornamentation is carried by a sculptured brass bacchant. 18″ high. The Christian Brothers Collection.

invest from five to thirty dollars for this decorative accent to your dinner service, then by all means use a small plate to protect the cloth.

Wine stains on cloth or napkins are unsightly, of course, and they're often difficult to remove, especially the stains of red wine. Here's a tip — use it at your own risk — for dealing with red-wine stain. As soon as possible, certainly while it's still moist, dab some white wine on it. The color is neutralized and the stain requires no further attention during laundering.

Removing the Cork

Opening a bottle of wine, even champagne, doesn't have to be a burdensome chore. If your bottle of wine has a screw cap, of course, or a crown cap like a soda bottle, it's a simple task.

Premium-quality table wines are always closed with a cork. This seals the bottle along the entire length and circumference of the cork, while a cap presses against only the mouth of the bottle. And, with red table wines particularly, the cork in a properly stored bottle permits aging of the wine to continue and thus becomes one silent symbol of product quality.

Still, it's the cork that intimidates many people, sometimes with reason. If the cork is dry, it tends to crumble when pierced by a corkscrew, and fragments of cork inevitably fall into the bottle. There isn't much you can do about the dry or otherwise deficient cork. If it comes out in segments, you may even find yourself in sheer desperation pushing the final chunk into the wine. Be glad it doesn't happen too often.

Right
A rich example of the late-nineteenth-century German silversmiths' art, this lovely covered goblet, crowned with a warrior in full regalia, is richly embossed with landscapes, masks, and festoons of fruit. 13" high. The Christian Brothers Collection.

Opposite
In this beautiful seventeenth-century Dutch still life by Abraham van Beyeren, elegant glasses are used as decorative accents. Oil on canvas. 55" × 46". M. H. de Young Memorial Museum.

A happy hunchback is shown dancing with a glass and a jug of wine in this etching by Jacques Callot from the series I Gobbi, *1622. The Christian Brothers Collection.*

Opposite
An early-sixteenth-century engraving by Albrecht Altdorfer depicts a knight in full armor serving bread and wine. The Christian Brothers Collection.

A normal cork, moist from sustained contact with the wine in horizontal storage, should be no problem at all. If you watch the waiters in a restaurant that caters to wine drinkers, you'll notice few if any failures with the corkscrew. They've had enough experience to become adept. But don't feel singular if you lack their dexterity. In The Christian Brothers collection at The Wine Museum are some of the many hundred corkscrews that Brother Timothy has assembled in the almost forty years that he has been applying his knowledge to the creation of elegant California wines and brandies. Each of those corkscrews is a testament to the frustrations of some innovative person who despaired of the openers previously available to him.

The most accomplished waiters seem to use the corkscrew that folds like a pocket knife and has, in fact, a knife blade whose sole purpose is to cut the foil cap on the wine bottle just below the lip. It's generally less expensive than the mechanical marvels that are available, and will last a lifetime once you master its use. First, with the blade, cut cleanly through the foil at the first indentation below the lip, removing the "cap" but leaving a clean-edged collar of foil around the neck of the bottle. Some practitioners of this tribal rite recommend that at this point you wipe the lip of the bottle with a clean napkin.

Next, insert the corkscrew in the cork, being careful to center the entire spiral, not the point, over the cork. When all the spiral has disappeared, position the notched end of the lever "blade" on the lip of the bottle, wrap a finger or two of your free hand around the braced lever, and raise the other end of the tool. The cork should slide out readily.

The hard-core ritualists call for a second wiping of the bottle mouth at this point. But if you're not afraid to live dangerously, you're at liberty to defy them.

Other Bottle Openers

It remains now to pour and drink the wine, but first a few words about other types of openers. One screw-type has a collar that automatically centers over the cork, and twin levers that rise as the corkscrew is turned. When they reach the limit of travel, all you need do is lower them and the cork comes out. Another self-centering device has twin screws, one that goes into the cork, another that lifts it. Surely the most baffling is the opener with two thin strips of metal that you slide down the neck of the bottle on opposite sides of the cork, then twist, and out comes the cork.

Champagne Cork

Opening a champagne bottle (which must be well chilled beforehand) is a totally different procedure, strictly a hand operation. First, remove only enough of the foil cap to get free access to the twisted wire hood that holds the cork in the bottle against an internal pressure of carbon dioxide that reaches seventy pounds or more per square inch. It's best, of course, not to agitate the bottle and precipitate a premature launching of the cork. Untwist the wire retainer until the hood is loose enough to remove. Holding the bottle at about forty-five degrees with its mouth near the first glass to be filled (and making sure it is not pointed at anyone), grasp the mushroom top of the cork in one hand and the body of the bottle in the other. Slowly but firmly, turn the bottle while holding the cork fast. Turn only in one direction. When the bottle turns free of the cork, be ready to pour, for often when the cork is removed, the first gush of wine is a flood. Opening the bottle in this fashion minimizes the danger of the cork flying off, and usually the wine behaves better. This procedure also usually tones down the loud "pop" that many associate with sparkling wines.

Opposite
In the past, tankards were frequently used as wine-drinking vessels. In this seventeenth-century Dutch etching by Cornelis Bega, a man enjoys his drink while sitting on a barrel. The Christian Brothers Collection.

ostgz

It is not always possible to budge the cork by hand. When it's obstinate, a pair of wide-mouth pliers will usually get it started, but be especially sure here not to direct the bottle toward any person. The same procedures and precautions apply to the bottle with a plastic stopper.

There's a ceremonial touch, with or without the "pop," to opening a bottle of sparkling wine, and you serve it promptly to avoid loss of the bubbles before they accomplish their purpose. Still wines, on the other hand, and especially red wines, usually should be opened a few minutes to half an hour in advance to let them breathe. No tragedy will befall the wine if you fail to make that allowance, but people with sensitive palates are convinced that a brief period of exposure adds a measure of improvement to the taste. That being so, you're not likely to be opening at least the first bottle of wine while your guests are at the table.

The First Sip

The custom — which you're at liberty to observe or defy — is to pour the first sip in your own glass, swirl it around, sniff it, observe the color against the light, then taste it. The purpose is to be sure the wine is sound. The chance that it won't be is pretty slender, but the custom is still worth preserving if only because it gives the host a dividend that he may scale to his own fancy.

Whether you serve the ladies first and thus make two trips around the table, or take your guests in the order of seating, is a small decision that rests entirely with you. There are solid precedents for both forms of hospitality. In either, the lady of the house or the guest of honor should be served first. The manner of serving additional portions is also optional. Except in expressly formal dinner parties, you should feel free to walk the bottle around the table or ask the guests to pass their glasses.

When to refill? There is, of course, no rule, but there is sharp division of opinion. One school says, don't pour another portion until the guest has drained his glass, because he knows his capacity and you may in a surfeit of hospitality embarrass him into exceeding it. The other says, pour whether the glass is empty or not and the guest will tell you when he has had enough. The ideal answer probably lies in your familiarity with your guest and his habits. Your choice of procedure is not likely to give you black marks, anyway.

Should you use a serving basket? It no longer serves anything more than a decorative purpose, and it really isn't much of a decoration. Time was, as noted earlier, when wines (and especially the reds) threw off a sediment after they were bottled. Cradled in a serving basket, the bottle could accumulate the harmless but unsightly sediment on an inner edge of the bottom. Then, if the basket was tipped gently for pouring, the sediment would stay there. California wines rarely have that shortcoming now, nor do the foreign wines of good quality. Nobody will fault you if you put to use the wicker serving basket or silver cradle in your possession. It may even give your table setting a touch of nostalgia.

Choosing the Wine

Given the wine service, what about the wine? From the thousands of possibilities, how do you choose the wine most suited to the occasion, or most complementary to the food? For long years, wine connoisseurs, real and fancied, maintained the tyrannical posture that choice of

*A man is shown drinking wine from various glasses
while seated in an arbor in this sixteenth-century
engraving attributed to Hendrik Goltzius.* The
Christian Brothers Collection.

wines was circumscribed by rules having the weight of law. It turned out, though, as it was explained in Chapter VI, that the only rule that really matters is the one that says, "Drink the wines you like best."

Firmest of the old "rules" was: "red wine with red meat, white wine with white meat and fish." This heritage supposedly reached our shores from Europe, where wine is less a beverage than it is a way of life. In Central Europe, there is available little fish and fowl, little white meat, but lots of cattle to make beef a dietary staple. And there, contrary to the "rule," a great amount of white wine is drunk with that beef.

Or, consider Italy, a country with an abundance of seafood and poultry, plenty of white meat, yet her predominant wine is red. In wines, the color line, in few words, is blurred. Consider instead a guideline. Your aim is compatibility of food and wine to the end that neither overpowers the flavor of the other. In practical terms, that means that a full-bodied or strongly flavored wine may overpower a very delicate dish. That's why a dry white wine probably is more compatible with a light seafood or chicken, or a robust red wine more compatible with a flavorful beef roast.

Rationalization of serving temperatures has also been subject to misinterpretation. Here again, the aim is not slavish conformity to a rule but the serving of wines at temperatures that emphasize their finest qualities.

"Room Temperature"

Actually, some of the confusion over serving temperature results from the introduction of central heating systems that significantly raised "room temperature." Before central heating, room temperature was surely no higher than sixty-five degrees, and seventy is probably the highest level at which a red wine will show off to advantage. Today, regulated indoor temperatures are seventy degrees or higher, and at that level, red wines suffer a taste handicap. The thing to remember is that room temperature when it was first applied to wines meant "cool room temperature" to bring out their finest flavor.

It hardly needs to be added here that if you like them at actual room temperature, or if you prefer them chilled, no one can rule you out of order. The rationale of the "cool room temperature" preference is that most of us don't like red wines chilled because there is some natural substance in a red wine, partly tannin in all likelihood, that makes the wine less palatable when it's too cold.

On the other hand, there are some red wines that were made to be served cold. They're the sweeter types, the *vinos*, in which the residual sweetness makes them more pleasant to taste when they are chilled. Sparkling Burgundy, as red as its still counterpart, is drunk only when it is chilled.

White wines are much better chilled. An hour or two in the refrigerator is enough to bring a still white wine down to optimum serving temperature, and it will usually stay cool enough through dinner without resort to an ice bucket, which is a cumbersome thing in most private homes. The sweeter white dinner wines, by the way, tend to taste better with a little more chill than the dry whites.

Again, though, there's another side to the story. In some areas of the world, notably including Germany, people frequently drink white wine in cool weather without additional chilling. They find that the real charm of the flavor and aroma emerge when the wine is not too cold. If this apparent ambiguity tells us anything, it is that individual preference is as much a prime consideration in serving as it is in one's choice of wine.

Forty-five degrees is not too cold for Cham-

*Throughout the wine countries during the warm
seasons, the cool wine cellars have traditionally
been favorite places for cheerful gatherings of
people, as is here depicted in this late-eighteenth-
century Italian hand-colored line engraving by
Giovanni Volpato (after Francesco Maggiotto).*
The Christian Brothers Collection.

The sure, satiric eye of English caricaturist, Thomas Rowlandson, is evident in this hand-colored etching, dated 1787, depicting a breakfast before the hunt. Here he pokes fun at the activities of the English aristocracy. The Christian Brothers Collection.

An anonymous mid-nineteenth-century English artist depicts a post-hunt alfresco meal accompanied by wine in this hand-colored etching. The Christian Brothers Collection.

In Le Chasseur Hollandois (The Dutch Hunter) *a hunter sits at the window holding a glass of wine. This 1773 line engraving by François Anne David is after a drawing by Aert Schouman of a painting by Gabriel Metsu dated 1661.* The Christian Brothers Collection.

pagnes and other sparkling wines, including the Sparkling Burgundy, and two or three hours in the refrigerator will usually pull them down to that level.

Sensory Responses

More as an aside than a guide, it may be noted that professional wine tasters who oversee the testing and blending functions in a winery never chill the wines under examination. They always taste at cellar temperature, which is probably fifty-five to sixty degrees. Even with white wines, which we think of as requiring a chill, the tasters claim they get a more authentic sensory response at cellar temperature.

Probably because wines have the appeal of moderation, they are winning acceptance in some uses that have been regarded as the private preserve of distilled spirits. Increasingly, the three-martini lunch of the business executive is yielding to a taste for wines both before and during the meal. Ideal for the purpose is a chilled white wine perhaps with a hint of sweetness like the Chénin Blanc produced by some forty-four California vintners, or a Riesling, a Chablis, or the proprietary Château La Salle of The Christian Brothers. These, of course, are table wines.

In a somewhat different category at cocktail time are the dessert and aperitif wines, which include, in addition to sherry, port, and Madeira, such popular wines as the vermouths, a number of very rich German wines made from grapes that were almost raisins before they were harvested, and some sweet or Haut Sauternes and Barsacs. Brandy also plays an important role in the transition.

More than any other dessert wine, sherry is commanding a position in the cocktail competition, even to the point of being served in cocktail glasses. For people wanting an appetizer before lunch or dinner without the jolt of a highly alcoholic drink, the dry or cocktail sherry can be a pleasant change of pace. Sweeter sherries, often identified as cream sherries, have won a great deal of popularity at afternoon or evening social gatherings.

Light Appetizers

Sherry is a versatile wine. Besides serving as an appetizer, or a substitute for the stiffer cocktail, it has been found to make an agreeable drink on the rocks with a couple of ice cubes, or as a "mist" over crushed ice with a twist of lemon.

A common characteristic of dessert wines is that they don't benefit from bottle aging. Some rare vintage ports are exceptions to this rule, but most port wines, including both American and foreign products, reach maturity in the cask. They're all considered dessert wines because of their natural sweetness, coming from grape sugar that wasn't allowed to be fully converted to alcohol in the fermentation process. Generally, the ruby ports, so called because of their brighter red hue, are sweeter, while the tawny ports are said to lose some of their color and

A betrothal banquet in seventeenth-century England is sensuously portrayed in this illustration from Henry Vizetelly's A History of Champagne, London, *1882. The Christian Brothers Collection.*

Opposite
La Santé Rendue (Health Restored) *is a late-eighteenth-century line engraving by Juste Chevillet after a painting by Gerard Terborch.* The Christian Brothers Collection.

sweetness through aging. Like the other high-strength wines, ports do not require horizontal storage. Quality dessert wines generally are stoppered with a flange cork, and their higher alcoholic content inhibits the deterioration that afflicts the more delicate wines when stored upright.

In this steel engraving by the German artist, Joseph Kohlschein (after a painting by Johann Peter Hasenclever), the wine tasters assemble in the vintner's cellar to evaluate the development of his wines. The Christian Brothers Collection.

The Vermouths

Although dry and sweet vermouths are known best in the United States for the flavors they impart to Martini and Manhattan cocktails, they also have achieved popularity on their own and with other beverages. Dry vermouth may be drunk as a chilled cocktail or over ice with a twist of lemon. In France it is sometimes mixed with Crème de Cassis, the syrupy essence of black currants, as a mild but extremely flavorful cocktail.

Like the dry, the sweet vermouth is really a flavored wine brought to a strength of 17 to 20 percent by the addition of brandy. Spices, herbs, and roots are combined for flavoring, and some of them — like the antimalarial agent cinchona — are credited with medicinal properties. Use of cinchona as an ingredient, in fact, probably accounts for the popularity of vermouth in the torrid equatorial zones.

A number of other apéritifs have enjoyed acceptance for many years. They are usually identified by brand name rather than type. Most of them are pleasant when drunk alone and chilled, and also combine well with spirits in cocktails. It's indicative of the American's insistence on creating his own taste patterns that these special European-born apéritif wines have never achieved in this country the standing they enjoy abroad.

Light Desserts

A dessert wine that should not be confused with the American wine of the same name is the sweet Tokay — the Tokaji Aszu — from Hungary. It's a white wine from the indigenous Furmint grape and is made and bottled in different degrees of sweetness that vary with the num-

ber of baskets, or *puttonyos*, of over-ripened grapes that are added to the must during fermentation. It is unique among white wines in that it improves tremendously with age to as much as thirty or forty years. (American Tokay, utterly unrelated, is a sweet dessert wine.)

The German dessert wines discussed in Chapter VI are in the same category and possess as

This early-eighteenth-century line engraving by Jean Baptiste Haussart (after a painting by Bartolomeo Manfredi in the French Royal Collection), shows a seventeenth-century drinking party. Note that the wine is poured from twine-covered flasks, similar to the modern fiasco of Tuscany, and that they drink from façon de Venise *glasses. The Christian Brothers Collection.*

Assemblee de Beuveurs.
Tableau de Barthelemy Manfredi, qui est dans le Cabinet du Roy.
Peint sur toile haut de 3 pieds large de 3 pieds 10 pouces grave par Jean Haussart.

well the Middle European heritage. Made from the latest possible harvest of grapes, fruit that ripened almost to raisins on the vines, they are ranked in increasing degrees of sweetness as Spätlese, Auslese, Beerenauslese, and Trockenbeerenauslese. Because of their rarity, they are usually high-priced and seldom classified as dessert wines; yet, because of their richness, they're not at all out of place with the sweets that

Dutch peasants are boisterously exchanging verbal views, stimulated by glasses of wine, in this eighteenth-century hand-colored line engraving by Englishman John Goldar (after a painting by Egbert van Heemskerck the Elder). The Christian Brothers Collection.

BOORS on POLITICS

La Vivandière

Soldats voila Catin.

J'ai pris part à tous vos exploits.
En vous versant à boire.

Songez combien j'ai fait de fois,
rafraîchir la victoire.

Wine was included in the rations of Napoleon's army, as can be seen in this early-nineteenth-century lithograph by Jean Henri Marlet entitled La Vivandière, Soldats voilà Catin (The Sutler Girl, Soldiers, Here Comes Katie). The Christian Brothers Collection.

232

Students are shown enjoying each other's company, and perhaps singing songs, while drinking wine in this anonymous early-nineteenth-century German line engraving. The Christian Brothers Collection.

conclude a dinner. Just a few ounces constitute a normal serving for sniffing and sipping.

Sweet Sauterne wines, although not classified as desserts, retain enough natural sugar to make them palatable with a sweet dessert or as an accent over fruit salad.

Versatile Beverage

Brandy is neither apéritif nor dessert wine, but as a pure derivative of the grape it merits attention in any evaluation of the uses of vinous products. It's additionally relevant in a California milieu because that state, with its abundance of the best grapes for brandy, French Colombard and Thompson Seedless, is the hub of American brandy production. The Christian Brothers are recognized as leading producers of beverage brandy and innovators in the technology of distillation and cask aging.

Brandy is a beverage of many uses. It may be sipped before, after, or without a meal. It may provide the lift for a tall, iced drink such as brandy and soda, or brandy and tonic water. It blends well in cocktails that usually call for whiskey or other distilled spirits — the Old Fashioned, the Manhattan, the Sour, the Gimlet, the Collins. Brandy, because it is derived from fruit, is more compatible than all other liquors with foods and drinks containing fruit. It blends well with lemon in the Sour, with the grape-derived vermouth in the Manhattan, and is splendid over sliced peaches or fresh strawberries.

Along with its contribution of flavor, brandy can create a spectacle to behold when poured over a food and ignited as a flambé. Most cookbooks contain recipes for crêpes suzettes, cherries jubilee, and other flambé dishes. The trick in getting the flame going is to use good brandy. Don't be too stingy with it, and be sure to warm it first. A safe way to warm it is to immerse the bottle of brandy in hot water for a short time. The brandy should be flammable at seventy-five to eighty degrees, but it is safer if you bring it up to a hundred degrees or so.

Popularity Scale

It hardly needs mention that the special brandies of the Cognac and Armagnac districts of France are universally popular with people who enjoy the aromatics released into the bowl of a snifter that's cupped in the hands. And, it isn't

In High Living at Bath, *an illustration in Vizetelly's* History of Champagne *(London, 1882) after Thomas Rowlandson, the love of excess prevalent in eighteenth- and nineteenth-century England is emphasized.* The Christian Brothers Collection.

HIGH LIVING AT BATH

(After Rowlandson, in the *New Bath Guide*).

likely that the famous brand-name Cognacs will be replaced in the affections of hard-shell devotees. Nevertheless American brandies have been moving up the scale of popularity through the use of select wines, the technique of continuous distillation, and the extended aging in small oak casks, which allows for a lighter and more consistently pure distillate. In this respect, the American product presents a distinct advance. By blending carefully chosen casks of continuously distilled brandy with well-aged heavier products of the traditional copper pot-still, The Christian Brothers now produce a limited edition of a special sipping brandy with taste and aroma characteristics rivaling those of the world's best.

The French are understandably proud of their brandies, and since 1909 have restricted the use of Cognac as a name to only the brandies produced in the two counties that constitute

In this two-tone lithograph by Englishman Joseph Nash from his mid-nineteenth-century series, Mansions of England in the Olden Time, *a pompous dinner is accompanied by fine wines in the Prescence Chamber of Hampton Court, Middlesex.* The Christian Brothers Collection.

the Cognac region. But France also produces many inferior brandies, some of them the result of a vintner's determination to squeeze the last drop of alcohol from his fermented grapes. Ordinarily, brandy is the distilled essence of wine. Economy-minded vintners distill not the wine but the residue from winemaking by cooking the pomace. This is the marc of the French, and the grappa of the Italians. Some of it is drinkable, but some is pretty raw and harsh. Regardless of its taste, it is subject to the same tax imposed on all distilled spirits, which makes it less of a price bargain than it appears to be.

Wine in the Kitchen

It's not the purpose of this work to serve as a guide to the use of wine in the kitchen or the medicine cabinet. Excellent tracts on both subjects, wine in cookery and as an aid to health, written by well-qualified experts, are available and are recommended for thoughtful study. A

During the mid-eighteenth century, corrupt English politicians staged dinner "treats" with ample wine, women, and song for their lower-class constituents. Occasionally these got out of hand. Here William Hogarth in this hand-colored etching depicts such a "popular orgy" promoted by the New Interest faction in the heated election of September, 1752. The Christian Brothers Collection.

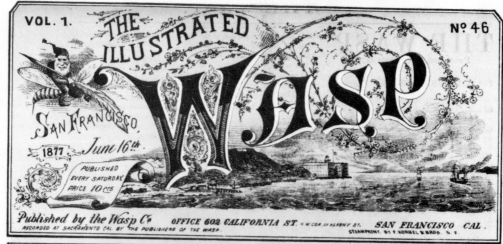

"THE RIGHT OF WAY"

Opposite
During the late nineteenth century a temperance movement was active in California, and George Frederick Keller produced a series of color lithograph cartoons satirizing the movement for The Illustrated Wasp. *The practitioners of the movement were always represented as ducks. Here in* The Right of Way, *the temperance fanatics are chased away by Bacchus, who arrives on the front of a locomotive named* Common Sense. The Christian Brothers Collection.

Die volle Flaschen, macht leer Taschen (*Full bottles make for empty pockets*): Overindulgence can lead not only to financial distress, but also to personal discomfort; thus, moderation is highly recommended in this line engraving published in the early eighteenth century and probably also engraved by *Joseph Friedrich Leopold.* The Christian Brothers Collection.

Two drunks are shown returning from the inn in this pencil and watercolor drawing by the late-nineteenth-century Frenchman, Eugène Grandsire. The Christian Brothers Collection.

HENRI QUATRE AND LOUIS SEIZE:
"Ventre St. Gris! *Is this my grandson Louis?*"
Illustration from A History of Champagne *by
Henry Vizetelly, London, 1882.* The Christian
Brothers Collection.

few words about these uses, however, may help
you decide whether you wish to explore these
topics in greater depth.

Obviously, the function of wine in the
kitchen is to flavor the food. But the constituents of wine and not the alcohol impart the
subtle flavor accents. The alcohol serves mainly
as a catalyst, the transmission belt that delivers
the taste of the fermented grape to the food.

In days when wine in cookery was the gus-
tatorial province of the affluent, milord and
milady sometimes found the kitchen staff, their

thirst too well slaked, unequal to their appointed
tasks of cooking and serving and of burnishing
the silver. To steer them away from alcoholic
perdition, a special cooking wine was com-
pounded that discouraged surreptitious dram-
ming. The simple solution was to salt the wine
heavily.

Good wine is no longer abused in this fashion,
and the kitchen staffs that oversee the use of
the bottle are overwhelmingly today the members of the family rather than uniformed servants. Instead of a bottle of "cooking" wine,

they're likely to use what was left from dinner last night or pour a few ounces from a jug of everyday dinner wine. Although it's generally accepted that good quality in a wine used in cooking is never wasted, a rare varietal premium wine really deserves a more dignified destiny.

Heat used in cooking dissipates the alcohol; since the alcohol is only the catalyst, anyway, it doesn't matter. What does matter is that heat also dissipates the flavor of the wine, thus de-

An early-seventeenth-century engraving by Crispin de Passe the Elder illustrates the themes of temperance and moderation. The Christian Brothers Collection.

Jets Over Alles: *Today is today; Bacchus rules the world. Watercolor drawing, dated 1823, by A. J. van Eyndhoven (after Jacob Smies).* The Christian Brothers Collection.

feating your purpose in using it. This accounts for the fact that recipes calling for wine specify that it be used at a late stage in the cooking. If certain soups that pick up a taste flourish from a dollop of sherry are permitted to simmer too much after the wine is added, the desired effect will be nullified.

A number of foods demand specific wines. A coq au vin needs a good red wine, for it becomes a part of the food. A duckling prepared in certain ways requires either a sweet wine, like a sherry, or a liqueur. The important thing to remember is, for optimum results follow the instructions in the recipe. Julia Child's

Mastering the Art of French Cooking is as authoritative in its citations of the use of wine as in the other aspects of her art. You'll find many other excellent works of this genre in the bookstalls.

Wine and Health

"Wine may be conducive to a longer life," writes Dr. Salvatore P. Lucia, thereby endearing himself to an entire industry from grape grower through wine-shop retailer, not to mention those of us who enjoy wine but never found a scientific rationale for our sipping.

His cheerful words appear in the book, *Wine*

242

This engraving by the seventeenth-century French artist Jacques Lagniet from a series illustrating proverbs is entitled, De fol, d'Enfant, et d'Yurogne, Garde toy, et t'en Éloigne. (From Fools, from Children, and from Drunkenness Beware and Stay Away). The Christian Brothers Collection.

A scroll-carrying dog is the subject of this early-twentieth-century Meissen porcelain wine bottle. The inscription on the scroll reads: Le vin est nécessaire pour égayer la vie, Il nous donne de courage, de la force et de l'esprit. *(The wine is necessary to cheer up our lives. It gives us courage, strength and wit.) 10¼" high.* The Christian Brothers Collection.

and Your Well-Being, one of several on the relation of wine and health that Dr. Lucia has written since 1948. Published in 1971 by Popular Library, the book is available in both hardcover and paperback. As a practicing physician and faculty member since 1931 at the University of California School of Medicine in San Francisco, Dr. Lucia has given the subject a good deal of professional attention and produced some startling analyses.

Champagne, he reports, is beyond comparison as the friend of the bride. It's used to toast her future at the wedding reception, it curbs her nausea in pregnancy, and it's useful as a food after natural childbirth.

Dr. Lucia makes no pretense that the wine cellar is a pharmacopoeia for all man's afflictions, and in fact raises the storm flags against serving wine to an alcoholic or to patients with peptic ulcer, stomach cancer, pancreatitis, kidney infection, prostate and genito-urinary disorders, epilepsy, or patients taking barbiturates and other forms of pain-relieving medication. At the same time, he rejoices that wine has never been classified as a "health food" because, as he says, Americans tend to resist edibles that are "good" for them.

How Wine Benefits

Dr. Lucia does say, however, that he has found evidence supporting his belief in wine as a source of energy; that it aids digestion; that it acts as a euphoric agent, thereby adding psychological benefit to the therapeutic value of its physical effect; that it helps to achieve nutritional balance in the convalescent while serving him as a tranquilizer and gentle sedative; that, properly administered, it's equally effective in stimulating the appetite and reducing a patient's weight; that it brightens the diet of the diabetic. He sees wine — its intake guided by a competent professional — as the source of a whole catalog of benefits for the human heart, including the prevention of angina pectoris or minimizing the pain that accompanies an attack, the prevention and treatment of arteriosclerosis, the relief of apprehension and any discomfort that

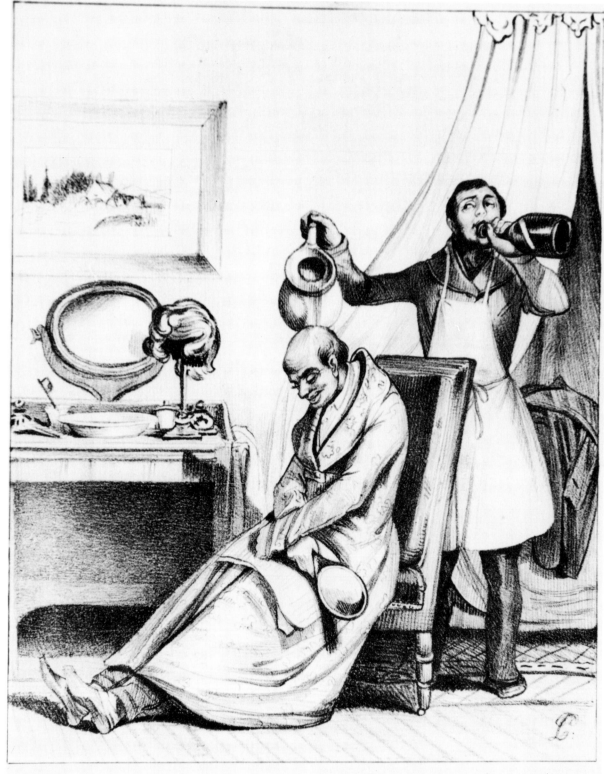

Deine Idee mit meinem alten Cognac ist vortrefflich, er stärkt die Haar
wurzeln, und ich werde nach deinem Rath täglich eine Flasche daran
wenden, damit ich die Perrücke bald entbehren kann.

might be associated with high blood pressure, and the prevention of coronary artery disease.

One reason we've been slow to establish the therapeutic values of wine, Dr. Lucia reports, is that an entire generation of American physicians lost touch with the medical lore of wine during the Prohibition years. But now many hospitals are serving wine with meals if the attending physician approves. Such hospitals found that wine service reduced patients' complaints by about 22 percent, boosted their morale, and gave them a rosier view of the attentions they received from the staff.

All these attributes, Dr. Lucia writes, "make wine not a cure-all but an accompaniment to graceful and intelligent living."

A more fitting salute would be hard to find.

Opposite
A humorous barber scene is the subject of this
mid-nineteenth-century lithograph by an unidentified
German artist. The caption reads in translation:
"Your idea for my old brandy is excellent — it
strengthens the hair roots. I shall follow your advice
to spend a bottle on it daily so that I shall soon be
able to do without my wig." The Christian Brothers
Collection.

Index